Flying the Flag

My career with Nuffield, Leyland and Marshall Tractors

To Nick

Christmas 2012

With best wishes

Tony.

Flying the Flag

My career with Nuffield, Leyland and Marshall Tractors

TONY THOMAS

FARM POWER
PUBLISHING

FLYING THE FLAG

MY CAREER WITH NUFFIELD, LEYLAND

& MARSHALL TRACTORS

First Published 2012

Copyright © Tony Thomas 2012

ISBN 978-0-9567019-2-3

A catalogue record for this book is available from the British Library.

FRONT COVER:

Tony Thomas, *left*, and Brian Webb, appeared together on the front cover

of the original 1964 sales brochure for the Nuffield 10/42 and 10/60 tractors.

© British Motor Industry Heritage Trust.

FRONTISPIECE:

The author ploughing with a Nuffield 4/25 tractor and a single-furrow Huard

reversible plough at a working demonstration in Warwickshire in 1968.

© British Motor Industry Heritage Trust.

PUBLISHED BY:

Farm Power Publishing

Wildrose Cottage, Reston Road, Legbourne, Louth, Lincolnshire, LN11 8LS, United Kingdom

www.farmpowerpublishing.co.uk

Cover design and book layout by Vertebrate Graphics, Sheffield.

Printed by Latitude Press Ltd.

Contents

Foreword

This is a very special book that all Nuffield, Leyland and Marshall tractor owners and enthusiasts will want to read. It covers the history of these tractors from the early 1960s and the controversial sale by Leyland Vehicles Limited of its UK tractor operations to Marshall of Gainsborough in 1982. It concludes with the unexpected collapse of Marshall in September 1985 and the subsequent but unsuccessful attempts to keep the tractor range alive.

This book will also be of great interest to anyone keen to learn more about UK tractor development during this period. Technical advancements made by competitors Ford, Massey Ferguson and to a lesser extent International Harvester and David Brown were virtually mirrored in the Nuffield, Leyland and Marshall tractor lines over the years.

I believe this unique book to be the very best and most accurate chronological account available, since it has been carefully compiled and written by Tony Thomas. Tony forged a crucial link between Nuffield, Leyland and Marshall's tractor sales, design and manufacturing departments and the dealer network and operators, both in the UK and overseas for nearly 30 years. His memoirs and supporting photographs bear testimony to his sound judgment, determined approach and keen attention to detail.

Born and raised in Nottinghamshire, Tony was interested in farming from an early age. He completed a course in general agriculture at Brackenhurst Agricultural College near Southwell, Nottinghamshire. After a further seven years of on-farm experience operating tractors and farm machinery, Tony sought to progress his career in the farming industry.

His father, who worked as a sales manager in the car division of T. Shipside Limited, the distributors of Morris, Wolseley, Riley, Vanden Plas and MG cars and Nuffield tractors in Nottinghamshire, heard of Morris Motors' plans to increase Nuffield production and recruit new members of staff for its agricultural sales division.

He mentioned these plans to his son and in October 1961 Tony seized his opportunity and applied for a job with the company. He was successful and in January 1962 he joined the Nuffield tractor sales office in Cowley and was appointed a UK area sales manager in September of that year. This may not seem significant, but it was the first time a qualified specialist in agricultural tractors and farm machinery had been employed by the sales division.

At that time, Nuffield tractors were being assembled at the Tractor & Transmissions plant in Birmingham where the production capacity was limited. There was little need for vigorous marketing and the small sales organisation was able to cope relatively easily. This was soon to change when the British Motor Corporation (BMC), the amalgamation of Morris Motors with Austin, was encouraged to build its new truck, tractor and diesel engine facility at Bathgate, West Lothian, Scotland, rather than its much preferred location in the West Midlands.

Suddenly, selling the higher volumes that were rolling off the Bathgate assembly lines became much more challenging. It is this challenge that particularly gripped the Nuffield tractor sales and marketing team as production soon began to outstrip demand.

Tony's strengths were especially recognised by Bob Turner. Bob had been brought in from Ford's tractor operation at Basildon as tractor marketing manager by Lord Stokes in 1968, when the ailing BMC organisation was merged with Leyland Motors to form British Leyland. Nuffield tractors were subsequently relaunched in 1969 with a change of name to Leyland, a new two-tone blue colour scheme and updated styling. An immediate and very encouraging sales bounce followed, but sadly this was not sustained over the longer term.

To augment the efforts of the design team and to improve the specification and scope of the tractor range, Tony was asked by Bob Turner to take on specific sales engineering tasks in addition to his normal duties. These included the design of a retro-fit hydraulic rear linkage assistor ram; an alternative to the Leyland transmission, leading to the introduction of the 262H and 272H tractors with faster tillage gears; reassessment of the specification of both the four- and six-cylinder tractors, with suggested improvements; and strong input into the final ratios selected for the world acclaimed Synchro gearbox.

Tony and I worked together on many of the strategic marketing and engineering developments described in this book and it has been my privilege to write the foreword for his story.

Brian Webb
Nuffield and Leyland tractor operations, 1963-1982.

Introduction

How many of us, I wonder, start work on a project, perhaps in our spare time, expecting it to keep us occupied for a few days, perhaps a week or two or maybe even a few months at most.

Well, way back in the early part of 2002 I embarked on what I thought would be one of those short term projects. It started after I had a telephone call from a young man who I'd spoken to on a number of previous occasions, but at the same time had never got to know really well. Yes, we both shared a common interest in the agricultural scene and in tractors, in particular. Over the years we had shared anecdotes, exchanged the odd photograph or piece of tractor literature but we had never reached the stage of forming any sort of working relationship.

Be all that as it may, this particular telephone call was from Rory Day who just a year earlier had been appointed editor of a new magazine – Classic Tractor – dedicated to tractors built since the 1960s.

Now at that time Classic Tractor was so new that I had to confess to Rory that I hadn't yet seen a copy. However, we chatted for a few minutes about this and that, when, without any form of warning or explanation or indeed without even putting the subject into the form of a question, he suddenly said "By the way I've put you down for our next Memory Lane series".

The title Memory Lane is, of course, self explanatory and what was being discussed was my involvement in the second of the magazine's long-running series, the first having been the memoirs of Mervyn Spokes who had worked for Ford tractor dealer Gates of Baldock in the retail side of the industry. I remember feeling quite flattered that here I was, several years into my retirement and largely out of touch with most things agricultural, being asked to contribute articles in one of the leading specialist tractor periodicals.

In spite of the fact that writing autobiographical articles of this type was a little outside my field of experience I felt I could hardly decline the invitation, if that is what it was, and so during that initial conversation we discussed details such as the length of each article and who would provide what in the way of photographs. Rory also undertook to send me one or two back copies so that I could get a feel for the type of approach and the subject matter in the first series of Memory Lane.

It is often said that one picture is worth a thousand words and in that respect I was very fortunate that I had retained quite a large collection of photographs going right back to my early days with the agricultural division of the British Motor Corporation.

Many of these proved to be invaluable memory joggers as I began to put pen to paper in order to meet Rory's first deadline. And as I did so, I was thinking that if this was the first instalment, then the last one would be in three or at most four months time. I couldn't have been more wrong.

My series of Memory Lane articles kept me occupied for just under four years. The writing of every single one provided me with a lot of enjoyment and it was nice to learn that many readers of Classic Tractor found them interesting, informative and thought provoking as well. After the series finally came to an end in 2006, quite a few people commented that the next stage should be to compile all the various instalments into a book.

So here it is! *Flying the Flag* is the story of my career working for one of *the* iconic ranges of British engineered farm tractors. This story, however, is not just about farm machinery – it is also about some of the tremendous people I had the very good fortune to work alongside during my almost 30 years with Nuffield, Leyland and Marshall. I hope you will enjoy reading it as much as I have enjoyed writing it.

Tony Thomas
Beckingham, North Nottinghamshire, May 2012.

Rolling back the years on Brian Prime's highly original Nuffield 460 during a Classic Tractor magazine photo shoot near Uttoxeter in Staffordshire in 2009.

One
First Step
on the Ladder

My name is Tony Thomas and I was born, brought up and educated in and around the city of Nottingham. I was born in 1937, just two years before the outbreak of the Second World War. During most of that time of grim conflict my family lived in Worksop, a medium-sized town in north Nottinghamshire. Fortunately, we were far enough away from Nottingham and Sheffield and other industrialised areas not to have to worry too much about the effects of the German air offensive, although I can remember talk of their bombers passing over Worksop on their way to create havoc in the steel-making areas of Sheffield.

In 1946 my family moved to Gedling, at that time a small village on the outskirts of Nottingham. Travelling east out of the village through the wide valley of the river Trent you would come to the Trent side village of Stoke Bardolph where, in my early teens, together with like-minded friends, I spent many happy hours fishing.

Fishing trips to Stoke Bardolph were in many ways an introduction to life in the country. Looking back, it was this, perhaps as much as anything else, that persuaded me to say to the principal at the Beckett Roman Catholic Grammar School in West Bridgford where I had spent five years which took me up to O level grade, that I had thoughts of wanting to become a farmer! With little more than that, the career wheels were set in motion and details of various agricultural colleges and universities were supplied to me by that diligent headmaster.

The first requirement of any agricultural college was a minimum of one year's experience of practical farming. So, on leaving school in the summer of 1954, I went with my father to see Arthur Cope of Manor Farm in Stoke Bardolph. Quite under-standably, Mr Cope was a bit dubious of this young man who had never held a pitchfork or been anywhere near a cow shed in his life! However, it was agreed that I would start the following Monday on a month's trial. And thus began what was a totally new experience for me and for any member of the Thomas family.

Manor Farm extended to around 100 acres and was rented from the Nottingham City Corporation. The Corporation owned several thousand acres along this part of the River Trent, most of which they farmed themselves, but the real and original reason for this land ownership was for sewage disposal purposes. The Corporation was responsible for the treatment of all the waste from the city of Nottingham before it could safely be discharged into the Trent.

Mr Cope had three brothers, two of whom had farms in the nearby villages of Burton Joyce and Lambley; the third brother in the partnership ran a small but very busy butcher's shop in the nearby town of Netherfield. Nearby, this shop had its own small slaughter house, also family owned, and here stock from the three farms and those purchased at local livestock markets were processed for sale in the shop. The Copes' business was a truly family owned and run affair; one thing I remember well is that during the run up to the Christmas period Mrs Cope and her two sisters-in-law would congregate in the large kitchen at Manor Farm, where they would spend several days making and baking dozens of pork pies for sale in the butcher's shop in Netherfield. Two of the Copes' farms had dairy herds and the third, Harlow Wood Farm at Lambley, was mainly arable, together with a decent-sized flock of sheep. The three farms were worked together so I experienced quite a wide variety of farming operations, from milking with the Alfa-Laval bucket units at Stoke Bardolph to hay-making with a Fisher-Humphries stationary baler. We harvested wheat using an Albion binder behind an old Fordson model N, or Standard, as they were better known.

Endless days were spent carting sheaves and stacking, often working with an experienced old hand at the end of summer thatching the stacks. The Cope brothers owned their own Marshall threshing drum, which meant many weeks spent threshing and baling in the late autumn and early winter months. No prizes for guessing who was nominated to work in the chaff hole!

In the autumn of 1955 I enrolled as a general agriculture student at Nottinghamshire College of Agriculture at Brackenhurst, near Southwell. Back in the mid-1950s Brackenhurst was a small educational unit with a total of approximately 45 residential students. The college was dedicated to training farmers' sons and daughters and people like me who wanted to get a foot on the first rung of the farming ladder.

BELOW LEFT:
Rolling out the milk churns at Manor Farm, Stoke Bardolph, near Nottingham, in August 1958. During my late teens and early 20s, I gained valuable first-hand knowledge on three mixed farms in Nottinghamshire.

BELOW RIGHT:
TRX1, the very first prototype Nuffield tractor, at Nuffield Mechanisations Limited, Ward End, Birmingham, in May 1946. The flowing side panels never made it into production.
© *British Motor Industry Heritage Trust*

Oddly enough, one of the aspects of life at Brackenhurst that has been of tremendous value to me in my working life in the tractor industry was an introduction to public speaking. I remember being a member of a four-man team which competed in the annual inter-dormitory public speaking competition. Our team was victorious that particular year and having been nominated as the 'speaker' I had entitled my speech 'A Typical Farmer Butcher'. My first 12 months of experience working for E. J. Cope & Sons was proving invaluable in more ways than one.

The year at Brackenhurst passed quickly, concluding with a two-week study trip to Sweden. Little did I realise at the time that I would become a regular visitor to this country in later years, in pursuit of export sales for the tractor range with which I eventually became involved.

After Brackenhurst I returned to the Copes and continued life as a farm worker. Modern machinery began to creep into their fleet; they were one of the first farms in the area to buy a combine harvester – a brand new trailed Ransomes with a 5ft cut. To drive the combine they bought a Fordson Diesel Major, also brand new, complete with a six-speed gearbox and live drive PTO. At the time this was one of the more modern tractors on the market and complemented the family's Fordson model N and three petrol/paraffin Fordson E27Ns. An Allis-Chalmers Roto-Baler was purchased to cope with the combined straw, but what headaches we had trying to stack those early round bales! All this equipment came from Fordson main dealer of the time, C. P. Evinson of Mansfield.

After a couple of years at Manor Farm, the ever thoughtful and considerate Arthur Cope began to wonder if I was gaining a sufficiently wide experience. So that I could keep pace with the latest developments in farm machinery it was arranged that my employment would be transferred to neighbouring Nottingham City Farms, which, in total, extended to over 1000 acres. Stoke Farm, as it was known locally,

Nuffield prototype TRX1 hoeing mustard with a Bettinson rear toolbar at Tinsleys of Holbeach, Lincs, in May 1946. Testing was carried out on farms near the Birmingham factory and also in Northamptonshire and south Lincolnshire.
© British Motor Industry Heritage Trust

had a large fleet of Field Marshall Series I and II tractors, some Marshall crawlers and a whole host of Ferguson TE-20s, with each driver having his own tractor.

There were no combine harvesters at Stoke Farm when I first joined, so the 20 or so farm workers were kept fully occupied in the summer with binders, stacking and then threshing. There were a couple of pick-up balers, one of which I think was an engine-driven Bamford Long and the other a McCormick International. This same workforce was kept busy in other seasons in large acreages of sugar beet destined for the local factory at Colwick. Apart from drilling the crop and steerage hoeing everything else was done manually, including singling and harvesting.

In spite of the reason for my move to Stoke Farm, I regularly received calls to do relief milking work and progressively, perhaps by default, became a full-time cowman with the pedigree herd of around 120 Shorthorns. Tractor work was limited to carting fodder to outlying stock and similar general duties. It gradually became apparent that my career opportunities were, rather than increasing, diminishing and my dream of climbing the farming ladder was as far away as ever. So what to do? I was in my mid-20s and hard decisions needed to be faced.

Ever since our move to Gedling some 17 years earlier, my father had been the car sales manager for T. Shipside Limited, the distributors of Morris, Wolseley, Riley, Vanden Plas and MG cars throughout Nottinghamshire. He was based in their showroom headquarters at Nottingham, but the company also had branches in Newark, Worksop and Loughborough. In these towns, Shipsides also had agricultural machinery depots selling, among other things, Claas combines, New Holland balers and Nuffield tractors.

In his capacity as car sales manager, my father came into regular contact with people from the Morris factory at Cowley and it was through these contacts that he came to learn of the plans to expand the production of the Nuffield tractor. This was to involve the transfer of production from the traditional home of the Nuffield models at the Ward End factory in Birmingham, known as Tractor and Transmissions or

The second Nuffield prototype, TRX2, was put to work with a parallel motion tool bar on Captain Bomford's farm at Fladbury, Worcs, in July 1946.
© *British Motor Industry Heritage Trust*

T&T for short, to a brand new manufacturing facility which was being built at Bathgate in the central belt of Scotland. Increased production was to be complemented by a big increase in staffing levels, particularly in the sales and service departments.

Both my father and I considered this as an opportunity worth exploring, and so it was that in the late summer of 1961 I wrote to the home sales manager for Nuffield tractors, providing him with a brief outline of my seven years of experience in the farming industry. As a result, I was invited to Cowley for a series of interviews with both Tom Cummings, who was in charge of sales in the home market, and his immediate superior, Leslie Bowles, the general sales manager.

Tom Cummings was a pleasant, mild, gentlemanly person; Mr. Bowles, however, was large in stature and somewhat forbidding in nature, particularly to a young farm worker who felt not at all at home in the finely appointed, carpeted offices of the British Motor Corporation.

I must have made some sort of an impression because a letter dated 16 November 1961 arrived from Tom Cummings offering me a position, initially in the sales office at Cowley, at a starting salary of £13.10s per week and with a start date of 1 January 1962. Decision time was definitely upon me, but had I declined that offer I would not now be starting to write about my involvement with one of the greatest names in the British tractor industry. My last day of work with Nottingham City Farms was on Boxing Day, 1961 and Robin Stone the general manager wrote to me on the 21st of the month, extending best wishes for happiness and success in the career I had chosen. I still have that letter together with the career-changing one from my new boss to be, Tom Cummings.

When I joined the British Motor Corporation in 1962 I was the proud owner of my own car, a shiny black Austin A30. However, it was decided that to get to Cowley for my first week's work with the company I should take the train from Nottingham to Oxford. Of course, at that time, 1 January wasn't a bank holiday as it is now, so my official start time in the Nuffield Tractors sales office was 8:30am on New Year's Day.

Changes were constantly being made to the prototypes. Note how the front cowl of prototype TRX2, pictured in July 1946, now resembles that of the production model.
© *British Motor Industry Heritage Trust*

Many people today will not be aware of the size and scale of the company which I was joining. The British Motor Corporation (BMC) was born out of the merger, in 1952, of two of the UK's largest, British-owned automobile manufacturers. First was the Nuffield Organisation, based in Cowley but with factories in Birmingham, Abingdon, London, South Wales and other parts of the country and abroad. It was developed out of the original Morris Car Company, founded by William Morris, later Lord Nuffield. Second was the Austin Motor Company, another major volume manufacturer of cars and commercial vehicles and based at Longbridge to the south west of Birmingham.

Within the sales department at Cowley were separate offices for the sales managers of such famous car marques as Morris, MG, Wolseley, Riley and Vanden Plas together with Morris Commercial Vehicles and, of course, for the Nuffield tractor. Home sales manager Tom Cummings and his assistant Mike Warland occupied the Nuffield office and it was here that I was to work for the next four months.

Shortly after my arrival, Tom Cummings became president of the Agricultural Engineers Association and his duties in this important position within the British tractor and agricultural machinery manufacturing industry meant that he spent more time away from the office than in it. It seemed strange to me that, although there were thousands of new cars everywhere as they streamed off the Cowley production lines, there wasn't a single tractor to be seen. The reason for this was, of course, very simple – the manufacturing base for the Nuffield tractor was in Ward End, Birmingham. It occupied the original Wolseley car factory, built at a time when the Wolseley Car Company was an independent operation, before it was taken over in the mid-1930s by William Morris as he expanded his business empire and before the manufacture of the up-market Wolseley range was transferred to Cowley.

At the time I joined the company, the Ward End factory was known as Tractor and Transmissions or T&T. Not only did it house the Nuffield tractor production line, but it was also responsible for manufacturing a large range of transmissions, gearboxes and rear axles for the Morris range of cars and commercial vehicles. You will hear more

BELOW LEFT:
Nuffield prototype TRX2 underwent field trials in 1946 fitted with a parallel motion tool bar of the company's own design.
© *British Motor Industry Heritage Trust*

BELOW RIGHT:
Nuffield prototype TR6 was equipped with a half-track system of in-house design. This TVO version was one of two produced for evaluation in 1946/1947.
© *British Motor Industry Heritage Trust*

about the important role played by T&T in the history of the Nuffield tractor, and about the dedicated people that worked there in support of the product later in my story.

However, since it is now well over 60 years since the introduction of the Nuffield tractor, a few facts about its early history might be of interest. The Nuffield tractor was launched in 1948, born out of a government desire and a national need in those early post war years to increase the production of home-grown food at the fastest possible rate. No doubt there was also a commercial wish on the part of Morris Motors to be involved in what was seen to be a huge growth industry. The manufacturing and assembly processes for tractors were not, after all, very much different to motor cars or commercial vehicles. William Morris's factories were among the most skilled and efficient in the world at producing these vehicles.

There is little doubt that the first move would have come from the government in the early months following the end of the war. There is also little doubt that a design and development team was drawn together very quickly. Interestingly, Doctor Merritt, who was also involved in design work for the David Brown tractor of a similar period, was appointed to a senior position within the team. I believe this explains why both tractors had a form of chassis to form the back bone of the tractor, rather than a stressed sump, which virtually every other design of tractor relied upon.

Much of the early prototype testing was done on farms around Birmingham and later on the estates of the Duke of Bedford in Northamptonshire and in south Lincolnshire. The name Nuffield would have been settled on at an early stage; Nuffield is the name of a village in Oxfordshire where William Morris had his home, Nuffield House.

There are two schools of thought as to why the 'Universal' designation was used; the first was that the new tractor should be capable of working with implements from any manufacturer, rather than needing a tailor-made range, as was the case with the

The Nuffield Universal Four, or 4DM as the diesel version was known within the company, was produced from 1957 to 1961. It had a high specification for the time. © *British Motor Industry Heritage Trust*

Ferguson System. The second was that the Nuffield would be designed and built in such a way that it would be suitable for any market, anywhere in the world.

There is probably an element of truth in both theories. The former, however, might be more difficult to substantiate in the modern world of trade descriptions and sales of goods acts, particularly as the Nuffield's relationship between its PTO shaft and the three-point linkage was always a little different to that found on other tractors.

In the case of its suitability for world markets, the Nuffield was designed with ease of routine and major servicing very much in mind. Uniquely, the entire hydraulic system was completely demountable from the rear of the tractor. Similarly, the clutch and/or the engine could be removed without the need to split the tractor. These benefits were rarely experienced as the Nuffield quickly established a reputation for reliability and durability that justly earned it the title of the Rolls-Royce of tractors!

The specification and general engineering of the first Nuffield proved to be a major advance in tractor design. It had a side valve TVO engine rated at a little over 40hp, a five-speed transmission (plus one reverse), an off-set steering wheel and sliding hub rear axles, together with two tricycle front axle options and modern styling. These features helped it to set market-leading standards. These revolutionary levels of sophistication were quick to be appreciated as the new model began to come off the Ward End production line and appear on British farms during the early months of 1949.

Looking back to those early days in the Nuffield sales office at Cowley, it is quite remarkable the changes that have taken place within the industry generally and within the tractor business in particular.

As a junior working in the sales office in the early months of 1962, much of my time was spent on routine office work. I well remember having to calculate, on a monthly basis, the UK percentage market share achieved by Nuffield and its four main competitors (Fordson, Massey Ferguson, International Harvester and David Brown) as the registration figures came in from the Agricultural Engineers Association. So what, you might say? Well, it is difficult to believe, but there was no such thing as

Sometime in mid-1962 I drove this Nuffield 460 from Ward End to Jack Green's farm at Coleshill to do some fieldwork. I was accompanied by Martin Stokes on a Nuffield 342.

a calculator, much less a computer, back then. All the figures were worked out with a pencil on paper and I suppose a certain amount of brain power. The fax machine had not been invented, much less the e-mail or any form of mobile phone; apart from land line telephones the only other means of communicating with other factories in the group or with customers abroad was by telex – by the standards of 2012 a very cumbersome and time-consuming system.

Another recollection is being introduced to the gentleman who occupied the office next door. He worked in car sales promotion and had tragically been totally blinded during the war while serving as a Wing Commander with the RAF. In 1961, accompanied by a co-driver who, no doubt, acted as navigator, he drove the MG model of the time, probably an MGA, at 100mph down the runway of a local Oxfordshire airfield.

The late 1950s and early 60s were the beginning of the halcyon days of the UK tractor manufacturing industry. Not only were British farmers buying in excess of 40,000 new tractors a year, British manufacturers were exporting more tractors than the rest of the world put together. There was hardly a country anywhere in the world to which the Nuffield was not exported. At the same time Nuffield was experiencing a healthy demand for its tractors in the UK.

Assistant sales manager Mike Warland would spend much of his working day on the telephone explaining to UK distributors why our delivery time against new orders was in the region of 16 weeks. In spite of the fact that the Birmingham factory at Ward End was working at maximum capacity, with full overtime, there was nothing he could do to improve on the delivery time. Maximum capacity at Ward End meant that about 400 tractors were produced per week and 70% of those would be destined for the many export markets.

Behind the wheel of a Nuffield 342 at the Public Works Exhibition at Southport, Lancs, in May 1962. This was one of my earliest drives on a Nuffield.

Another fact that is difficult to believe today is that at the time, British farmers had only five major brands to choose from: Fordson, Ferguson, David Brown, International Harvester and Nuffield. A few high-horsepower North American tractors were available, John Deere being one, along with Fordson conversion manufacturers such as County and Roadless. The UK market was still blissfully unaware of names such as Fiat, Same, Deutz, Fendt, Renault, Zetor, Belarus and Valmet. How times have changed.

Other aspects of the tractor market have also changed. The Nuffield 4/60 and 10/60, both rated at 60hp, were among the most powerful tractors available at

RIGHT:
Nuffield's reluctance to join the four-wheel drive market prompted Italian importer Cantatore of Turin to develop its own conversion, fitted here on a Nuffield 460.

BELOW LEFT:
Members of the Nuffield team at the 1962 Royal Show at Newcastle upon Tyne, from left: Val Muir, Gordon Barratt, Mike Keogh and myself.

BELOW RIGHT:
Rated at 60hp, the four-cylinder Nuffield 460 was one of the most powerful tractors available on the British market during the early 1960s.
© British Motor Industry Heritage Trust

that time, and four-wheel drive was virtually unheard of in this country. During my first weeks at Cowley I remember being asked by Tom Cummings if I had any thoughts on four-wheel drive tractors. I could only base my comments on my experiences with the Fordson E27Ns with which I had worked at Stoke Bardolph. They weren't renowned for their tractive ability, so I commented that four-wheel drive would seem to be quite a logical development.

Tom, however, said that although Nuffield had been field-testing four prototype four-wheel drives during the late 1950s and early 60s, the company had decided to pigeon-hole the designs as there was no real market for them. Sadly, I never saw any of these tractors and, as far as I am aware, none are still in existence although fortunately photographic records remain of them.

In view of the way the market has developed, what a fateful decision that was not to pursue four-wheel drive.

It is a fact that the UK market was probably the last in Europe to appreciate the benefits of four-wheel drive and at least one of Nuffield's export markets decided to go it alone in this respect.

Realising that they were not in a position to satisfy their customers' demands for a factory-built four-wheel drive Nuffield, the Italian importer and distributor of the time, Cantatore of Turin, decided to produce its own conversion. Over a period of several years in the early 1960s they converted several hundred Nuffields to four-wheel drive, many of which are still at work today on Italian farms. In much more recent times, one or two examples have been brought in to this country by enthusiasts to add to their collections of Nuffields.

At the end of April 1962 I transferred from Cowley to the Tractor and Transmissions factory at Ward End, to get some experience of the business in areas other than sales. Not only was this where the Nuffield range of two models (one four-cylinder and one three-cylinder) were produced, but it was also the home of the technical service, parts supply, design and engineering departments and the service training school. Just as with Cowley, these were not huge departments, but they were staffed by people completely dedicated to the product and to its customers.

Walter Rishworth, as service manager, and his assistant George Kipling headed up technical service; Norman Newton ran the training school and John Cochrane was in charge of implement approval. This latter section was interesting and had been established in recognition of the fact that Nuffield never had any intention of producing its own range of implements.

Instead, it was prepared to ensure, as far as possible, that any implement from any manufacturer was capable of being matched to the Nuffield. This was John Cochrane's responsibility as implement approval engineer. He would field-test machines submitted by manufacturers to assess their suitability to the tractor.

If changes were found to be necessary, the supplier would be informed, changes would be made and a retest carried out. If everything was then deemed to be acceptable the machine would be authorised to be fitted with a brass plate stating that it was 'Approved for use with the Nuffield tractor'. This approval was greatly valued by implement manufacturers of the time.

Two
Nuffield Sales

One of the first people I met following my move to T&T was Martin Stokes. Martin had joined the Company on 1 January 1962, exactly the same date as I did, but he had gone direct to T&T to be schooled in the technicalities of the Nuffield tractor. I first came across him in the service training school working with Norman Newton, who was in overall charge of product training.

On leaving school, Martin had done an agricultural machinery apprenticeship with machinery manufacturer Wilders of Wallingford. Like me, he applied for a job with Nuffield after hearing of the expansion plans for the range with the planned move of production from Birmingham to Bathgate, Scotland. At the time of our first meeting, Martin, having already worked for four months in the service school under Norman Newton, was already technically very knowledgeable about the two current models in the range – the 342 and 460. By the way, these were the first two models not to carry the 'Universal' badge; from thereon it had been decided that the model designation system would give an indication of some aspect of the specification of the tractors to which they referred. In the case of the 342 we had a tractor with a three-cylinder engine producing 42hp and with the 460 it was a four-cylinder power unit developing 60hp.

Norman Newton was an absolute master of product training. He made no attempt to pull the wool over the eyes of his students and openly acknowledged that here or there, the product might have one or two problems.

However, by the end of any of his courses, he had created so much enthusiasm for the product that his students left convinced that the Nuffield was, without doubt, the finest tractor on the planet!

Martin had undergone this drip-fed indoctrination for four months by the time of our first meeting but, like me, he had very little working field experience with either of the two models in the range.

At this time, the Nuffield 342 and 460 were coming towards the end of their production life. They still had the original Nuffield five-speed transmission design, which had served the tractor very well for 14 years, keeping it ahead of the competition as far as gear ratios were concerned. However, to maintain its competitive edge, chief

TOP:
Nuffield's Universal Three is put through belt-pulley tests at Nebraska. Fuel consumption readings were also recorded at the same time.
© *British Motor Industry Heritage Trust*

CENTRE:
Official performance tests were carried out on the Nuffield Universal Three at the Agricultural Engineering University of Nebraska in 1958.
© *British Motor Industry Heritage Trust*

LEFT:
Nuffield and Austin's stand at the 1962 Royal Highland Show was a mightily impressive affair.

designer Bill Whatton and his team had been working on a development that would double the number of forward gears from five to ten and provide two reverse ratios.

One day – it was mid-May – Martin and I were told to drive two tractors with these new transmissions out to the farm of Jack Green at Coleshill to try them in the field. For secrecy reasons both tractors, which were really pre-production Nuffield 10/42 and 10/60 models, were badged as the 342 and 460.

We took a Howard Rotavator with the 10/60, probably a 70in model, and behind the 10/42 we had a three-furrow Ransomes plough. Thus we both gained our first real live field experience with the tractors that were to become a major part of our working lives for the next 20 or so years.

Martin went on to become a highly competent and completely dependable service engineer, much liked and respected by colleagues, dealers and farmers across the UK and in several export markets. Sadly, he died in 1992 following a short illness, just before his 53rd birthday.

What of the other T&T personalities with whom I came into contact? Perhaps some readers will remember the two original UK service engineers of that time: Eric Seymour-Harris worked with distributors south of a line from Bristol to the Wash, and Bob Overton performed the same duties in the rest of the UK. Both had come up through the ranks, having started work with Wolseley Motors as apprentices.

One of the real characters was assistant service manager George Kipling. It could truly be said of George that what he did not know about the product was certainly not worth knowing. At each Smithfield Show he would be seen walking from his hotel to Earls Court together with Eric Harris, both resplendent in white shirt, company tie, rolled umbrella and, to top everything, each would be wearing a carefully brushed bowler hat! In spite of this, or perhaps because of it, George played an important part in the successful development of the Nuffield tractor.

BELOW LEFT: Nuffield's close affinity with the Austin Gypsy vehicle, both products of BMC, was promoted quite heavily at the 1962 Royal Highland Show.

BELOW RIGHT: Sectional tractors prepared by training school apprentices took pride of place on Nuffield's stand at the 1962 Smithfield Show in London. © *British Motor Industry Heritage Trust*

During the 1950s, 60s and possibly into the 70s it was critical to the commercial future of any tractor product that it had successfully completed an official performance test at the University of Agricultural Engineering at Lincoln, Nebraska. Several Nuffield models of the period were submitted for test, perhaps one of the earliest being a Universal Three in 1958. George Kipling and a young Bob Beresford were entrusted with the responsibility of representing the company for the duration of these arduous procedures.

Bob Beresford, who would have gone to Nebraska on more than one occasion, later rose through the ranks, becoming engineering director at Bathgate. During my time in Bathgate, of which much more further on, Bob and I had a number of disagreements, some quite heated, over several aspects of design and development. There were occasions when he seemed to think that he knew more about the specification requirements of the worldwide marketplace than those whose responsibility it actually was to identify those requirements and to bring them, through laid down procedures, to the attention of his engineering and design department. In years to come I experienced Bob's abrasive and sometimes aggressive management style but, in the end, common sense prevailed and in terms of product development, the sales and marketing department, of which I was a member, more often than not obtained the product changes they deemed necessary. It can be said, however, that Bob's experience of the product, starting as it did in the early days of T&T, enabled him to make an invaluable contribution to the development of both the Nuffield and the Leyland tractor.

Towards the end of May 1962 I was informed that I would be included in the sales team attending the Royal Highland Show the following month at Ingliston, Edinburgh. The Royal Highland Show was the first of the major UK summer events to find itself a permanent showground and the 1962 show, while not the first at Ingliston, was probably only the second or third. There were no tarmac roads, as now. When it rained, as it did that year, the main avenues soon became a sea of mud. Duck-boards had to be placed across the worst ground to provide access to many areas, including the Nuffield stand.

In common with those of other tractor manufacturers, our stand was a large and prestigious affair, and there was always great competition between the various companies. This would be the case not only with the quality of the build and appearance of the stand itself, but also in the quality and volume of the catering and general hospitality offered to visitors.

The theme of our stand this particular year was the association between Nuffield and Austin, which manifested itself in the form of the Nuffield tractor and the Austin Gypsy. Both were designed, developed and manufactured by the mighty British Motor Corporation and aimed mainly at agricultural markets around the world. Are there, I wonder, any examples of the Austin Gypsy still in existence? If so, it is to be hoped that they are receiving the same tender care as many Nuffield tractors do today. The Gypsy did not stay the course in the face of the longer established Land-Rover, but as is so often the case, users would tell you that it had many features superior to its only competitor of the time.

In spite of my involvement in a wide variety of aspects of the Nuffield tractor operation at both Cowley and at T&T at Ward End, Birmingham, I still retained a close interest in all things agricultural.

Much to the surprise and amusement of home sales manager Tom Cummings and assistant sales manager Mike Warland, I replied to an advertisement in the local Oxford newspaper from a local farmer who was looking for a weekend relief cowman. This involved two days milking with a herd of around 40 Friesians and Ayrshires on the farm of a Mrs Hitchens. It turned out that Mrs Hitchens, who was a Commander of the British Empire and a JP, lived at what I suppose might be termed the small stately home of North Aston Hall in the Oxfordshire village of Steeple Aston.

The pre-printed post cards on which she used to write to me stated that her number for both telephone and telegrams was Steeple Aston 200, and that the local train stations were Bicester and Fritwell. No doubt, today, North Aston Hall has at least a six-digit telephone number and while Bicester probably still has a railway station, it is most unlikely that Fritwell appears on the timetable of whichever company operates train services to that part of Oxfordshire.

It has to be said that neither Tom Cummings nor Mike Warland were particularly knowledgeable about farming in general, nor indeed about the type of work the Nuffield tractor was used for when it left the factory. In fact, I was probably the first person on the sales team to have any practical experience of farming. I could see no good reason for not keeping in touch with the world of real-life farming so for several months during the early part of 1962 I spent my weekends milking cows at Steeple Aston.

If my memory is correct, the 1962 Royal Show was the last to be held before it moved to its permanent site at Stoneleigh. The last of the roving Royals was held on

F. H. Burgess sold more Nuffield tractors than any other dealer. This Universal Three model was displayed on the company's stand at the 1960 Cheshire Show.

the Town Moor, Newcastle-upon-Tyne, and what a mammoth and expensive task it must have been to stage those huge shows at a different location each year. As was the case at the Highland Show of 1962, the stands of the five major tractor manufacturers were large and elaborate affairs, taking much longer to erect and demolish than the four or five-day duration of the show itself.

The full Nuffield sales and service teams attended the Royal Show, where the 342 and 460 models and the Austin Gypsy formed the focal points of the large and prestigious stand. The same tractor models were also featured at the 1962 Royal Smithfield Show, where again prestige and quality were always uppermost in the minds of the tractor manufacturers and their stand designers. The Nuffield stand at Earls Court had polished wood-block flooring, not the easiest surface for the sales and service teams to spend a long, arduous week talking to farmers and dealers for up to eight hours a day.

TOP:
A Nuffield Universal Four is loaded onto dealer T. Shipside's truck at BMC's Tractor & Transmissions factory in Birmingham. T. Shipside had depots at Worksop, Newark and Loughborough.
© *British Motor Industry Heritage Trust*

LEFT:
Photographed at the Ward End Works in Birmingham, this Nuffield 342 is equipped with Dunlop 12.4/11 x 28 Fieldmaster tyres.
© *British Motor Industry Heritage Trust*

The tractor display that year consisted of two 342s, two 460s together with a sectioned model of each plus, as a centre-piece, another 342 on a floodlit turntable. This was also completely sectioned and chromed so that it was possible to see virtually every moving part of the engine, clutch, transmission and hydraulics. These three sectioned units would have been prepared at the Apprentice Training School at either Ward End or Cowley or both, and they were an aspect of exhibition material for which Nuffield was justly regarded as the No.1 around the world.

Anybody who has worked at major shows will know that they are far from being an easy few days away from the routine of business life in the office. The Highland and the Royal were long, hard days, but the Smithfield was the toughest of the three.

Company discipline was always high; no excuses were accepted for being late on duty in the morning, which meant being on the stand by 8:45am at the latest. With the possible exception of the last day, you were required to be present when the national anthem was broadcast over the public address system at 6pm. Most evenings this was followed by a de-briefing meeting in the office, admittedly with a glass of your favourite tipple to help clear away the all-pervading dust that used to be a part of Earls Court in the 1960s and 70s. It was very often 7pm before you could escape into the not so fresh air of a London winter's evening.

Looking back down memory lane to the tractors of the early 1960s, British-built tractors appear to have been incredibly good value for money. As I have said before, at 60hp the Nuffield 460 was probably the most powerful tractor on the market, if only by one or two horsepower.

Yet its list price was only just over £800. Certainly, tractors then were not as sophisticated as now; in some cases you had a sack of hay for your seat cushion and I have heard drivers say that this same sack would be placed on the head when it rained, sleeted or snowed!

We are also talking about a time well before tractor cabs became the norm. Power steering was available as an option at around £45, but since most farmers employed tractor drivers, they saw little reason to add to the price of the tractor they were buying to make life any easier for the man doing the work. As a result very few tractors were sold with this option.

Since that time, of course, inflation has taken its toll and costs of add-on extras like quiet cabs have to be taken into account.

But it would seem fair to say that £800-worth of 60hp in 1962 would perform in the field every bit as well as the 60hp available from a tractor produced in 2012 – and at what cost to the farmer!

Forgive me for my nostalgia but I have a cutting in my records from the Daily Telegraph dated 14 February 1961, the headline of which reads 'Tractor output will be increased – Sunday working at BMC'. The first paragraph reads, 'Sunday working to meet the record demand for Nuffield tractors is to be introduced at British Motor Corporation factories which supply components to enable tractor production to be increased to record levels. British tractor manufacturers largely escaped the recession which hit the rest of the motor industry last year and exports increased to 146,287 tractors worth £86m. This compares with 1959 figures of 115,749 and £65.5m.'

Does something appear to have gone wrong along the way? I could express my own views, but perhaps this is not the place to do that and in any case I might be accused of being politically incorrect and nationalistic.

The Daily Telegraph article goes on to say, 'A Sunday morning shift would be worked in the machining section in the Tractor & Transmissions factory at Washwood Heath, Birmingham. A Saturday morning shift was already in operation. Production of Nuffield tractors had been increased to record levels and under the BMC £49mn development plan production would be moved to a new factory at Bathgate, West Lothian.'

BELOW LEFT:
The features of the Nuffield 3/45 and 4/65 models were explained in this 1968 salesman's data handbook, published by the Nuffield Press.© *British Motor Industry Heritage Trust*

BELOW RIGHT:
BMC's Nuffield Press subsidiary was responsible for producing the sales and technical literature for the Nuffield tractor. This 10/42 and 10/60 booklet dates from 1965. © *British Motor Industry Heritage Trust*

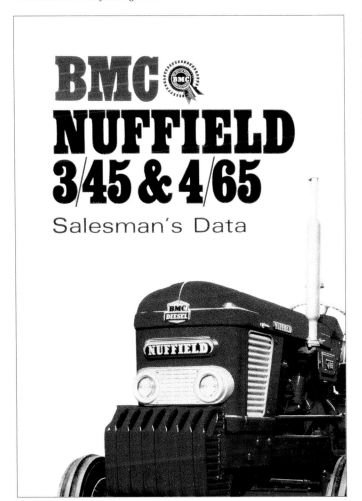

I can only hazard a guess at the levels of employment that such production figures created. Not only, of course, on the production lines at Ford, Ferguson, David Brown, International Harvester and Nuffield, but also at the numerous component suppliers. Every one of those tractors would almost certainly have been fitted with British designed and produced hydraulic, electrical and fuel injection equipment. Original equipment would also have included British-made tyres, the majority of which would have been made by Dunlop at their Midlands-based Fort Dunlop factories.

It is interesting to note that William Morris, later Lord Nuffield, and the directors of Dunlop entered into a 'Gentleman's Agreement': the former would use nothing but Dunlop tyres on any vehicle he produced and the latter would use nothing but Morris vehicles for all aspects of its manufacturing operation. This agreement remained in force for many, many years. Nuffield tractors produced at the Birmingham Tractor & Transmissions factory at Ward End would, without exception, have been dispatched to markets around the world fitted with British-made Dunlop tyres.

TOP:
Midlands dealer F. H. Burgess was appointed a Nuffield distributor after parting company with Massey Ferguson. This is the company's Hereford depot in the early 1960s, with a Nuffield 460 taking price of place near the main entrance.

RIGHT:
End of an era as the 94,033rd and last Nuffield tractor built at Morris Motors' T&T branch at Ward End, Birmingham, rolls off the line. The tractor, a 460, serial number 64T41481, was destined for Australia.
© *British Motor Industry Heritage Trust*

The agreement was marked each year at the Royal Smithfield Show by a small evening function known as the Dunlop Dinner and attended by sales and service personnel from each company.

This practice was still in force when tractor production was transferred to the new factory at Bathgate, long after the death of Lord Nuffield. This long standing agreement only became diluted with the demand for radial tyres; for some reason Dunlop was very slow off the mark with the development of what, at that time, was a new tyre specification. As a result, Bathgate had no choice but to begin using Goodyear, Kleber and, in some cases, Pirelli tyres. I wonder how many tractor tyres are produced in the UK today?

During my early months with the British Motor Corporation the huge scale of the company never ceased to amaze me. It was clearly not completely self-sufficient in terms of internal component supply, but it owned such companies as SU Carburettors, and two body-making companies, Pressed Steel Fisher, Llanelli, and Prestcold at Reading. A huge foundry at Wellingborough produced engine blocks, gearbox and hydraulic unit casings, and the massive Nuffield tractor chassis. The Nuffield Press in Oxford was responsible for every item of printed paper and all the photographic work required by the organisation, including brochures, price lists, driver's handbooks, parts lists and workshop manuals, not just in English, but in the many languages of the countries to which the products of the corporation were exported. Every item would carry the legend 'Printed by the Nuffield Press Limited, Cowley, Oxford, England'.

After the 1962 Royal Show it was planned that I would spend more time out of the office. For two or three months I travelled around the Midlands, the north of England and Scotland with Gordon Barrett, the sales representative for that area. He was approaching retirement and the plan was that, in due course, I would succeed him. Gordon had joined BMC about five years earlier and he, together with another area sales manager, John Hiatt, covered the whole of the country. Gordon had previously worked for BMC's rival, the Rootes Group, which produced the Hillman, Singer and Humber ranges of cars. At some time he had also worked for the manufacturers of the Turner 'Yeoman of England' tractor.

Mr. Barrett, as he preferred to be known, and I spent several months visiting distributors and dealers together. The standard company car of the day was the Wolseley 1500, a model recognised as having a good power-to-weight ratio and corresponding performance. Mr. Barrett was not the slowest of drivers, so we covered a lot of ground, visiting the companies whose livelihoods depended, in part at least, on the sale of the Nuffield 342 and 460 tractors.

Many of the dealers had been involved with the Nuffield since its introduction in 1948 and had been distributors or dealers for Morris, MG, Wolseley or Riley cars for a lot longer than that; in other words the early Nuffield tractor distributor network was formed, in large part, out of a loyal group of car retailers. Unlike today, it was an arrangement that worked extremely well, in most cases.

Most of these companies set up separate organisations, with premises and staff dedicated to handling the sales and servicing of the Nuffield tractor. They soon came into contact with machinery from a large variety of other manufacturers. As a result, many Nuffield distributors from the early 1950s onwards were involved with Claas combine harvesters, New Holland balers, Ransomes ploughs and Howard rotavators and often the range of equipment manufactured by Bamfords of Uttoxeter.

It is not necessary to mention them all, but some dealer names still stand out today and will doubtless be remembered by Nuffield owners of the time: Henry S. Tett at Faversham; Sycamores of Ramsey; Lowndes Garages at Carmarthen; T. Shipside Ltd in Nottinghamshire; Appleyard at Wetherby; Loxhams in Preston and Thos. Corrie of Dumfries. At that time the Kenning Group was also a big player in the agricultural machinery business, with Nuffield tractor outlets in Doncaster, Hull, Hereford and Shrewsbury.

With the exception of those in the south of England, I had business dealings with most of our distributors over the years and in most cases they were very cordial. However, one name in the south that can't go unmentioned is that of Central Garage at Leedstown in Cornwall. This was a family owned and run business and although it never came within my area of direct responsibility, until briefly in the late Marshall days, the husband and wife team that ran it, Hazel and Ken Hall, came to know most people within the organisation. Originally, I think, they handled the Fordson tractor on a sub-dealer basis but they had been involved with our franchise from the Nuffield days and they never missed a major national show and made a point of attending every dealer conference and every new product launch. I came to know them well and their enthusiasm for everything Nuffield, Leyland or Marshall had to be experienced to be believed; they sold many hundreds of orange, blue and Golden Harvest tractors and their reputation for service and customer care generally was second to none and an example to other members of the trade, no matter which brand of tractor they represented.

Following my initial induction period with Mr. Barrett, I remember that my very first solo visit to a distributor was to F. Keiser & Son of Penrith. This was a small company run by the son, also called Frank after his father, who founded the business. They were also Morris and Wolseley car dealers for the town and surrounding area, and I came to the conclusion that tractors were only of secondary importance to them. I suggested to Frank that I would remain in the area for a second day and that it would be a good idea to visit some of his tractor customers. This we did, driving around the north Lakes in Frank's big Wolseley 6/110 which seemed a bit incongruous in some of the small Lakeland farm yards we visited. Soon afterwards, Oliver & Snowdon at Carlisle and Haltwhistle became involved in the Nuffield franchise, rising quickly to become one of the most successful Nuffield/Leyland main dealers in the north of England.

Winding my way through the early 1960s, it is quite remarkable to think that the majority of tractor ranges available at the time each comprised only two or three models. There was Fordson with its Dexta and Super Major; Massey Ferguson with the 35 and 65; David Brown had the 770, 880 and 990; and Nuffield relied on the 342 and 460. International could manage three models with the B-275, B-414 and the B-614.

At the time of my visits to Keiser's, north-east England consisted of the two counties of Cumberland and Westmoreland; Cumbria was not even a twinkle in the eye of local government back then. Though not a big seller in the UK generally, the 342 was particularly popular in this part of the country.

Rated at 42hp, the 342 was, of course, comparable in terms of power output to the best seller of the time, the MF 35, but the 342 was quite considerably heavier by about 750kg (or nearly 15cwt in old money). This fact, coupled with the superior torque characteristics of the BMC engine (127lb ft compared to the 119lb ft from the MF 35's Perkins three-cylinder engine) resulted in the Nuffield being considered a safer, more stable and superior performer on the steep hills with which most farmers in the area had to contend.

When dealers Oliver & Snowdon took over responsibility for Nuffield and then Leyland sales in the area, the pattern of sales continued. This trend persisted when the excellent three-cylinder BMC engine was phased out and replaced in the three-cylinder Leyland 253 by the same Perkins three-cylinder engine used in the MF 135.

The extra weight of the Leyland tractor made far more efficient use of the 2.5-litre Perkins engine. The 342 was also superior in terms of hydraulic lift capacity. This was particularly useful at a time when buck-raking was becoming an increasingly common method of bringing in grass for the silage clamp. As a result, the 342 and its immediate successor, the 10/42, became particularly popular with hill farmers in various parts of the UK.

Having now been appointed as a fully-fledged area sales manager, my territory consisted of the north of England from Yorkshire and Lancashire upwards, together with the whole of Scotland and Northern Ireland. Gordon Barrett operated below this as far south as a line from Bristol to the Wash; south of this Midlands-ish area was the responsibility of John Hiatt.

All new company representatives were issued with a copy of the BMC Representatives Handbook, regarded as the bible for numerous aspects of conduct while out on company business. One or two quotes from this make interesting reading: 'It is essential when travelling on company business to appear in front of the contact neatly but conservatively attired and groomed, without ostentation. If travelling by company car, every effort should be made to ensure that it is clean, both inside and out, as this is often the customer's first and last impression of the representative.'

BELOW LEFT:
Members of the Nuffield team at the 1963 Royal Highland Show, from left: John Hiatt, Val Muir, Mike Keogh, Martin Stokes, Gordon Barratt and George Kipling.

BELOW RIGHT:
In 1963, I was joined in the Nuffield sales office by three new colleagues: Brian Webb, left, as demonstrator; Val Muir, centre, as sales manager for Scotland and Northern Ireland; and Mike Keogh, right, on sales in the south of England.

BMC's sales bible went on to add: 'When it is necessary to stay overnight, care must be taken to ensure that a suitable hotel is selected which will provide adequate meals and accommodation at reasonable prices. Whilst a three-star hotel in the city centre may charge £4 per night for a single room and breakfast, a similar hotel away from the city centre will charge £2.10s for the same sort of amenities.'

I remember that the standard allowance for a midday meal was 12s 6d or 52 1/2p in the coinage of today and petrol was just beginning to touch 4s (20p) a gallon. How times and values, both monetary and professionally, have changed over the last 50 years.

In February 1963, the above-mentioned Nuffield sales team was suddenly doubled in size. Gordon, John and I were joined by Mike Keogh, Val Muir and Brian Webb. Mike had previously worked with the Nuffield importer in Nairobi, Kenya, a company called Gayley & Roberts, and Val came to the Nuffield tractor operation after working for several years in various parts of Africa for the Colonial Service. They both brought with them a knowledge of farming and agriculture which, apart from myself, had been somewhat lacking in the sales department.

Brian Webb had completed a course in agricultural engineering at Lackham College of Agriculture in Wiltshire and was appointed to the team as a demonstrator. He brought with him a tremendous in-depth knowledge of many aspects of tractor and machinery operation and design, which was to prove invaluable in the coming years.

This increase in sales staff was implemented partly to take account of the expected increase in tractor production as the new manufacturing plant at Bathgate came on stream, and partly to take account of the fact that Gordon Barrett was approaching retirement.

As a result of the changes, John Hiatt relinquished his sales responsibilities in the south to establish a new demonstration department in which Brian Webb would play a major role.

Mike Keogh took over responsibility for sales in the south, while Val Muir, who was a Scotsman, replaced me in Scotland and Northern Ireland. I was assigned to look after Nuffield distributors in Yorkshire and Lancashire, and the Burgess Group, which by now had completed its break with Massey Ferguson and, depending on the area, represented either Nuffield or David Brown.

The transfer of Nuffield tractor production from T&T at Ward End to Bathgate in Scotland was carried out on a progressive basis. T&T first relinquished production of the three-cylinder 342, the first model to be built at the new Scottish factory. The 460 continued to be built at T&T for some time, until the production processes were fully and properly installed at Bathgate.

Sadly, precise dates for the last tractor off the line at T&T and the first off the new line in Scotland have not been recorded. It is known, however, that the last Birmingham-built 460 was the 94,033rd Nuffield to be built (apart from prototypes), that its serial number was 64T41481 and that it was an export model destined for Sydney, Australia. Is it, I wonder, still in existence?

Nuffields were regarded by many as the Rolls-Royce of tractors and as the last example of its era, tractor number 64T41481 will have undoubtedly held a special place in the hearts and minds of the skilled workforce at Ward End, Birmingham.

Three

From Birmingham to Bathgate

During 1961 and 1962, what might be regarded as the traditional home of the British engineered and manufactured Nuffield tractor – Tractors & Transmissions in Birmingham – was being wound down. At the same time, some 300 miles to the north, at Bathgate in West Lothian, a multi-million pound investment in a brand new production facility was approaching completion.

BMC's Scottish factory was conceived out of a joint plan between George Harriman, the then chairman of the British Motor Corporation, and the Labour government of the time, under Harold Wilson. The aim was to provide work in an area where jobs were in increasingly short supply, the result of the closure of coal mines and shale oil workings, both of which had reached the end of their economic lives. Rather more distantly, the ship building yards of central western Scotland were also facing increasing competition from the Far East.

Bathgate was designed to build not only the Nuffield tractor, but also a range of BMC commercial vehicles that included trucks between three and 26 tons, together with the three-, four- and six-cylinder engines that powered them.

Accordingly, the factory design incorporated three separate units known as A, B and C blocks. B block, located in the centre, produced the engines and C block housed the new tractor line. B block also housed what at that time was the largest machine shop in Europe, a facility dedicated to the in-house manufacture of a very high proportion of all the components required for tractors, commercial vehicles and engines.

The scale of the whole project was huge; it was built on what today would be described as a greenfield site.

It covered around 70 acres of farmland known locally as Moss Side Farm. At its peak, this new factory would provide employment for over 6000 workers from across the central belt of Scotland.

The UK distributor network was kept informed of the progress of this major development and in the autumn of 1962, some 80 distributors were invited to a conference held at the North British Hotel on Princes Street in Edinburgh.

The conference programme included a conducted tour of Bathgate to view the new factory, which was by this time approaching completion. A fleet of coaches also took visitors to see the new Forth Road Bridge, which was also under construction at that time; as I remember, the north and south towers were complete and the cables which would support the carriageways were being put in place.

As far as the Nuffield tractor was concerned, the new factory had a planned eventual output of 750 units per week. For the distributors, this meant a considerable reduction in the delivery times they had been experiencing throughout the life of the Birmingham-built tractors. It would give them, they believed, the opportunity to increase their sales around the world.

As I have already mentioned, the last Birmingham-built tractor, a Nuffield 460, was exported to Australia. The first Bathgate-built tractor, a Nuffield 342, did not go quite as far afield and was donated to Bathgate Town Council!

Production at Bathgate was gradually increased during 1962 and 1963, and in 1964 the 342 and 460 models were replaced by 10/42 and 10/60. These tractors had the same horsepower and traditional Nuffield styling as their predecessors, but came with, among other new features, a ten forward and two reverse speed gearbox. These new models also had self-energising dry disc brakes and a new independent, dual-flow hydraulic system fed by a Dowty twin-chamber pump. The price of the 10/60 at the time of its introduction was £860. This was one of the most powerful tractors on the market with a transmission providing more ratios than any of its competitors.

A glossy, full colour brochure was produced to mark the introduction of these two new models showing, on the front cover, a 10/42 being driven by Brian Webb and a 10/60 with myself at the wheel. One of the inside pages depicts a 10/42 fitted with a McConnel hedge-cutter, driven by Keith Argyle, another recent recruit to the demonstration team.

Location photography for the brochure took place on Jack Green's farm at Coleshill, where Birmingham-designed tractor prototypes had undergone many hours of testing over the years. We know now, in 2012, that the 10/60 with its registration number of 701 UJO is still in existence and in the careful ownership of Malcolm Williams of Whitland, Carmarthenshire. What, one wonders, are the chances of reuniting it with the 10/42, registration number 704 UJO, driven by Brian Webb?

This was one of the last occasions that Mr Green's farm would have been used for such work because the new transmission, brakes and hydraulics used on the 10/60 and 10/42 were among the last new Nuffield features designed in Birmingham.

At around this time, home sales manager Tom Cummings arranged that the team – Mike Keogh, Val Muir, Brian Webb and myself – should pay a visit to Bray Construction in Feltham, Middlesex, who had expressed an interest in fitting their industrial loader front axle to a Nuffield 10/60. They wanted to explore the viability of such a project with people who would help them promote sales into a marketplace with which they were not all that familiar.

The outcome of our discussions was the Bray 10/60, a 60hp tractor with equal-size wheels front and rear; Bray favoured either 12 x 38s or 14 x 30s. What this tractor lacked in manoeuvrability it more than made up for in terms of pulling ability!

The move to Bathgate included the relocation to Scotland of a considerable number of production and other personnel from the Birmingham factory. It also coincided with the approaching retirement of many of those in the design and development department, people who had long been responsible for keeping the Nuffield models competitive in the marketplace. Dedicated characters such as George Kipling, Walter Rishworth, Bill Whatton and John Cochrane were about to sever their links with the product that had been a major part of their working lives for many years.

What was not generally known at the time, certainly not to me in my capacity as area sales manager in 1964, was that a decision had been taken at main board level to employ the services of an outside design and development team to engineer future models of Nuffield tractors. My involvement and that of my counterparts in UK sales with this Coventry-based organisation would not begin until some 12 months later.

A little earlier in my story I mentioned George Harriman, chairman of the British Motor Corporation during my first few years working with the company's agricultural division. He remained in this position right up to the time of the formation of British Leyland in 1968. I never met him, of course, although in later years I did meet Sir Donald Stokes, albeit rather briefly.

I mention George Harriman at this particular point in my story because, during the 1960s, the British Motor Corporation was right at the top of the success stories within the many fields of British manufacturing. I have yet another press cutting from the Daily Telegraph of around 1962, reporting that the company was producing something like 18,000 cars, trucks and tractors a week – that is approaching one million units a year.

During that same period, exports were running at some 330,000 units per year and in the previous year the company exported £125mn worth of vehicles. Imports, on the other hand, accounted for by foreign components, were valued at a measly £2.5mn. The Daily Telegraph reporter commented: "How's that for a balance of payments?"

The board of BMC received the highest praise from the Daily Telegraph reporter. The three top men, George Harriman, together with production director Bill Davis

BELOW LEFT:
The brush guard, Cooke winch and dual wheels suggest this Nuffield 4/60, seen outside 'C' block at the Bathgate plant, was destined for a tough life overseas.
© *British Motor Industry Heritage Trust*

BELOW RIGHT:
This sectioned unit was produced to promote the introduction of the Nuffield 10/42 and 10/60 and was probably used for the first time at the 1964 Royal Highland Show.

and sales director Jimmy Woodcock, were all former company apprentices. In addition, another nine former apprentices were members of subsidiary boards.

I can't help but feel a tinge of nostalgia for the might of the industrial base of this country of ours at that time, and more than a tinge of sadness, to put it mildly, for the way it has been neglected and eroded in the intervening years. There are, of course, all sorts of reasons for this, but it might be worth enquiring how many of our present-day large manufacturing corporations are headed up by former apprentices of the company concerned; indeed, how many apprentices are undergoing training in such companies? I suspect not very many, if any at all.

As a footnote to the Daily Telegraph article, the reporter commented that at the time of his visit to BMC's Longbridge plant, "the local Birmingham paper was carrying 20 columns of jobs vacant ads".

The opening of the new Bathgate factory no doubt resulted, at least in part, in Nuffield tractors scoring a major coup in 1965. Up to this time JCB, the market leader for backhoe loaders, had based their units on the four-cylinder Ford tractor. JCB took the Ford skid unit, consisting of an engine, clutch, gearbox and back axle, and used it as a base for their world famous excavators.

Clearly, for some time top-level discussions had been taking place between JCB and BMC and these culminated with the announcement in 1965 that, forthwith, all JCB excavators would be based on a 60hp Nuffield skid unit, essentially the engine and transmission from the 10/60 tractor. This arrangement continued for many years and resulted in many thousands of skid units in a wide variety of specifications being produced in Bathgate for dispatch to JCB's factory at Rocester in Staffordshire.

Nuffield and later Leyland skid units were also supplied to companies such as Hymac, Coventry Climax (tough terrain forklifts), Bray (four-wheel drive tractors) as well as several companies in Italy and Scandinavia.

As Bathgate began to overcome the teething problems that were almost inevitable with the commencement of such a large-scale development, the sales team, then consisting of myself, Mike Keogh in the south and Val Muir in the north, Scotland and Northern Ireland, were initially tasked with increasing sales through the existing distributor network. At a later stage we were asked to strengthen the network with new appointments.

The new home of Nuffield tractors at Bathgate in Scotland begins to take shape around 1960/1961. The tractor assembly line was housed in 'C' block, seen here.
© *British Motor Industry Heritage Trust*

As far as existing distributors were concerned, we began to move away from the old boy sort of relationship. It had been almost the norm throughout the Tractors & Transmissions era, when tractors were in such short supply and delivery periods were so long. If a farmer cancelled an order because he felt he had been kept waiting too long, nobody lost too much sleep because there was always a queue of other customers more than willing to take the tractor.

But now, as a result of Bathgate coming on stream, this was all changing. The new, younger sales team began to take a more pro-active approach. They knew that in the Nuffield 10/42 and 10/60 they had excellent products; they also knew that like all their predecessors, these two models would not be outperformed in the field. They also knew that in terms of specification they were in first place. At 60hp the 10/60 was still one of the most powerful British-built tractors on the market; it also offered the most sophisticated gearbox and it was still the only tractor with a fully independent PTO.

Taking all this into account, several 10/42s and 10/60s were put into the field as demonstration models. We never had as many demonstrators as the mighty Ford organisation, which would virtually flood national events such as the National Plough-ing Championships with acres of blue tinwork (and some would say with black exhaust smoke!). In later years we came to know two of the Ford demonstration team very well. James H. Taylor subsequently moved from Ford to Nuffield and, following the formation of British Leyland, Bob Turner also moved from Ford to become sales director of our tractor division, with an almost direct line to Lord Stokes.

Despite the obvious differences in scale between Nuffield and Ford, we progres-sively developed a very professional approach to demonstrations, this effort being headed by Brian Webb and his meticulous eye for detail. Whether we were demon-strating to individual farmers, at dealer events or to a wider audience at large national shows (the latter more about image building) the name of the game was geared entirely to selling more and more tractors.

Those of us who were involved in the UK tractor business at that time were only just becoming aware of the increasing competition from overseas manufacturers. Brand names previously unheard of in the UK were beginning to make their mark. Zetor was one of the first foreigners to cross the channel, followed by Same, then imported by Cornish & Lloyds and later by Bamletts of Thirsk. How those little acorns have grown.

It is strange how some people become synonymous with a product. For many years, Mike Keogh, Val Muir, Brian Webb and myself, together with our colleagues on the service side, namely Bob Overton, Eric Harris and Martin Stokes, were looked on by farmers and distributors alike as the Nuffield team.

Other personalities came and went, never seemingly over-enthused by what we believed was the finest product in the market place. On the demonstration team, Brian was joined for quite a long time by Keith Argyle and for much longer than that by Brian Sneed, who left eventually to join Kverneland.

Ray Broadhurst joined us from Bamfords of Uttoxeter to become a demonstrator and was very quickly appointed to the sales team to supplement the work being done by Mike, Val and myself. I like to believe that those of us who stuck with the product worked as a good team, achieved the respect of those in the trade with whom we had regular contact, and did much to increase the popularity of the British-built products with which we were proud to be associated.

During the 1960s the British Motor Corporation was producing around 18,000 cars, trucks and tractors per week. This equated to almost 1mn units annually, with a high percentage of these going for export. Taking Nuffield tractors as a prime example, sales to overseas markets were rarely less than 75% of total production.

Unemployment at this time was low, probably lower in real terms than the figures we are asked to believe today. However, for the sake of discussion, let's say that the rates of employment are, for all practical purposes, the same.

As a nation we do not now export that many tractors, no combine harvesters or balers and, perhaps, just a handful of ploughs. The majority of tractors, cars, lorries and buses on our roads are imports made in France, Germany, Italy, Japan, Scandinavia and elsewhere.

We are agreed that just as many people are working today as there were in the 1960s. Obviously, far fewer of them are working on production lines as was the case in the 1960s, so what are they all doing? Working in shopping centres, call centres and leisure centres? If this is so, what as a result is being produced for consumption either in this country or, more importantly, for export? Not very much, is the answer.

Be all that as it may, it occurs to me that I haven't really said anything critical of either the Nuffield tractor as a product or of the company for which I was working. It is a fact that in the 1960s the British Motor Corporation was a highly successful multi-national operation. It is also a fact, as I have said once or twice before, that the Nuffield was looked upon, all over the world, as the Rolls-Royce of tractors. I think, therefore, I have been reasonably accurate in my portrayal of events so far.

Everything to do with the product and the company had, in large part, been sweet-ness and light. In the early to mid-1960s two factors came in to play to bring about a small change to this happy state of affairs. In writing about these some may say that I am under-estimating the effect these factors had on the Nuffield tractor and its stand-ing in the worldwide market place. Forgive me, but even after a period of nearly 30 years, I still feel a sense of protective loyalty to both the tractor and to the company.

The first of the above-mentioned negative factors concerns the move of tractor production from Birmingham to Bathgate. It is a fact that it took the brand new factory quite a while longer than it should have done to get to grips with quality control and to move towards the same high standards that we had taken so much for granted with the Birmingham-built units.

The manning of the factory involved the employment of people who had never experienced production line work. Consequently, major retraining programmes had to be implemented. It should also be remembered that there were, at this time, huge demands from all over the world for British-built tractors.

As far as Bathgate was concerned, at the same time as production was being increased to meet targets, management pressure was also being applied to ensure the prompt dispatch of tractors to customers. There was, amongst this flurry of activity, a temptation to allow tractors to leave the factory that should have spent rather more time in inspection and rectification than was the case.

The second factor resulted from the introduction of the 10-speed gearbox that heralded the launch of the 10/60 and 10/42. It should be remembered that at 60hp the 10/60 and its predecessor, the 4/60, were at the top of the horsepower tree in the UK. As such, they were popular throughout the arable areas of south-east Scotland, through eastern England and right down to the Thames. Their excellent pulling power earned them many supporters in parts of Yorkshire, Lincolnshire and Essex, to name but a few of the really heavy land areas.

Up to and including the 460, the final drive of the Nuffield had remained virtually unchanged; it had stood the test of time and seen several increases of power over the 16 years from 1948 through to 1964. To my non-technical mind this speaks volumes for the correctness of the original design.

The final drive utilised a massive pinion and bull-gear arrangement (one smaller gear with 11 teeth driving a big bull-gear with 46 teeth). With the introduction of the 10-speed transmission this was changed – not change for the sake of change, but a change made necessary to ensure that the new gearbox provided a good spread of ratios for slow-speed work. In theory this was fine, but at the same time draft implements were getting bigger and heavier. Bigger ploughs with more furrows (a four-furrow plough was still unusual at that time) and new-fangled reversible ploughs were becoming

TOP:
Nuffield's presence at the 1965 Highland Show was an impressive affair. Austin's ill-fated Land-Rover rival, the Gypsy, made up the stand numbers.

LEFT:
Nuffield's pro-active approach to demonstrations helped win over many customers. I used this Nuffield 10/60 and Bamford plough at a Cheshire ploughing match in 1964/65.

increasingly popular. Ransomes, with their British designed and built range, were far and away the leader in the plough market. Farmers were upgrading from the two-furrow TS82 to the TS83 and then to the completely redesigned and heavier TS103, which came to be regarded as the bench-mark reversible plough for several years.

Into this developing scene came the new Nuffield 10/60 with its new gearbox and its new final drive. Now, in my experience, every tractor manufacturer has had the odd problem model or two, and it is often these problems that live longest in people's memories. I will not seek to revive any of these memories other than to say that the nine-tooth pinion engineered for this new final drive was less capable of withstanding the stresses of mid-1960s heavy land arable farming than the 11-tooth version it replaced.

Working in the heavy land areas mentioned above, the Nuffield 10/60 suffered a fall from grace; while its proven power and pulling ability which we had known before was still undiminished, the nine-tooth pinion no longer ensured the inbuilt durability and reliability. In many other areas, both at home and abroad, the 10/60 and the 10/42 continued to be as competitive and popular as ever, and with improving availability from the Bathgate factory the sales graphs continued on a gradual upward slope.

Around the same time as the introduction of the 10/60 and the opening of the Bathgate factory, a decision was taken within BMC to centralise the whole of its product sales operations. Up until this time, the tractor division, under Tom Cummings and Mike Warland, had worked at Cowley with their counterparts from Morris Cars and Commercial Vehicles, Riley, Wolseley and MG.

They were moved to Longbridge, where they were located in the same office facility as the Austin sales team. It was a huge facility and housed rows and rows of secretaries, clerks, production programmers, allocators, progress chasers and many others. This was, of course, prior to the dawn of the computer age and virtually every piece of documentation had to be generated and processed by hand.

Nuffield retained the same familiar styling, typified here by a 1950s Universal Three, from 1948 right through until the launch of the 3/45 and 4/65 in 1967.
© *British Motor Industry Heritage Trust*

It was into this busy and bustling environment that a young Ron Kettle joined the office-based Nuffield sales team. Ron had recently completed a course at Harper Adams Agricultural College. Initially, like me, he was employed in sales administration; in later years, however, he was to play an important role in product training, demonstrations and export sales to some of the more difficult and far-flung markets around the world.

There were some really great guys at Nuffield during the 1960s. Invariably they were dedicated to the Nuffield tractor, enthusiastic about its sales potential, always helpful and rarely critical. Many distributors and names of individuals come to mind in this particular context; if some are not mentioned here, it is no way a reflection of the high regard in which they were held by myself and the company I represented.

Appleyard of Wetherby was one of our largest UK distributors. It was led by managing director George Ayres, together with John Lund and Harry Plummer, sales and service managers respectively. Appleyards also employed Dennis Lawn and Ken Wilks, two top-class salesmen. There were others, but sadly the passage of time has allowed their names to slip from my memory. Working together, they were responsible for the sales and servicing of many hundreds of Nuffield tractors across a wide area of the North and West Ridings of Yorkshire.

During the late 1960s Appleyards expanded its agricultural machinery operations, acquiring a Massey Ferguson distributor with branches in Thirsk and Ripon. And it wasn't long before the competitive franchise was ousted and replaced by Nuffield. Dealer staff who had been schooled in the art of selling Massey Ferguson products were also dedicated types; to expect them to convert, without objection or resistance was, and I suppose still is, expecting the impossible.

The existing manager at the Thirsk head office had accepted this situation and Brian Webb and I went up there to get to know his sales and service staff. It was our job to instill product knowledge and inject them with as much enthusiasm for the Nuffield tractor as possible. This was always a major challenge and on this occasion the manager advised us to 'bring big boots and bloody well use them!'

Brian and I were accustomed to using rather more subtle methods than that, but we knew where he was coming from. Massey Ferguson personnel were among the most difficult to re-educate – this applied all over the world.

Several years later in the early Leyland era, Ron Kettle and I experienced the same sort of resistance in Morocco, a country to which we had just exported 500 Leyland 270s. Our task was to change the allegiance of several small Massey Ferguson dealers, but more of this later.

Another incident that has remained in the memory occurred during a sales visit to T. Shipside Ltd's depot at Gateford Road in Worksop. Immediately after the introduction of the 10/60 and 10/42, I was in the office of Frank Driffil, their respected sales manager. Over the years, Frank had sold many, many Nuffields to the numerous large estates in north Nottinghamshire, north Derbyshire and south Yorkshire. North Notts is known as the Dukeries; in those days it was inhabited by affluent, well-connected farmers. I suspect not a lot has changed today, although some might disagree!

Back to Shipsides, where Frank Driffil was enthusiastic about the increased sales opportunities for the new models. He felt the combination of 60hp and ten speeds,

RIGHT:
Back in August 1964 you could buy top-spec versions of the Nuffield 10/42 and 10/60 models for £821 and £876 respectively.
© *British Motor Industry Heritage Trust*

BELOW:
The front cover of Nuffield's August 1964 price list and a typically colourful and attractive advert for the 10/42 and 10/60 tractors from the same year.
© *British Motor Industry Heritage Trust*

POWER - ECONOMY - QUALITY - RELIABILITY

NUFFIELD 10/60
The following prices are CARRIAGE PAID HOME

Basic Model
Equipment includes differential lock; hand brake; electric starter; swinging drawbar; disc steering brakes; engine and transmission oils; licence holder; radiator shutters and temperature gauge; 6·00—16 (4-ply) front tyres; 11—36 (4-ply) rear tyres 716 10 0

Standard Model
Equipment includes hydraulic power unit incorporating P.T.O. and with automatic depth control and independent hydraulics; linkage; electric lighting with twin dipping headlamps and horn; tractometer; de-luxe seat; differential lock; hand brake; electric starter; swinging drawbar; transmission steering brakes; engine and transmission oils; licence holder; number-plates; radiator shutters and temperature gauge; 6·00—16 (4-ply) front tyres; 11—36 (4-ply) rear tyres 818 10 0

De-luxe Model
Equipment as on Standard Model, but also includes independent P.T.O. 876 0 0

NUFFIELD 10/42
The following prices are CARRIAGE PAID HOME

Basic Model
Equipment includes differential lock; hand brake; electric starter; swinging drawbar; disc steering brakes; engine and transmission oils; licence holder; 5·50—16 (4-ply) front tyres; 10—28 (4-ply) rear tyres 661 10 0

Standard Model
Equipment includes hydraulic power unit incorporating P.T.O. and with automatic depth control and independent hydraulics; linkage; electric lighting with twin dipping headlamps and horn; tractometer; de-luxe seat; differential lock; hand brake; electric starter; swinging drawbar; transmission steering brakes; engine and transmission oils; licence holder; number-plates; 5·50—16 (4-ply) front tyres; 10—28 (4-ply) rear tyres 763 10 0

De-luxe Model
Equipment as on Standard Model, but also includes independent P.T.O. 821 0 0

OPTIONAL FITTED EQUIPMENT

	£ s. d.
All Models	
Belt pulley and guard	15 0 0
Drawbar extension	1 15 0
Drawbar offset extension	1 10 0
Rear wheel weights (pair)	10 0 0
Front end weights	9 0 0
Front wheel weights	6 7 6
Additional independent braking system	22 10 0
Vacuum braking equipment (conversion kit)	60 0 0
Radius rods	5 10 0
All 10/60 Models	
Additional front weight	7 2 6
Power-assisted steering	50 0 0
Heavy duty clutch	9 2 6
6·00—16 (6-ply) front tyres in lieu of standard	1 15 0
6·00—19 (6-ply) front tyres in lieu of standard	4 10 0
7·50—16 (6-ply) front tyres in lieu of standard	10 0 0
11—36 (6-ply) rear tyres in lieu of standard	6 10 0
12—36 (6-ply) rear tyres in lieu of standard	22 10 0
12—38 (6-ply) rear tyres in lieu of standard	25 10 0
13—30 (6-ply) rear tyres in lieu of standard	21 0 0
14—30 (6-ply) rear tyres in lieu of standard	30 0 0
11—36 (6-ply) Industrial tread tyres in lieu of standard	6 10 0
11—36 (6-ply) Universal tread tyres in lieu of standard	6 10 0
Twin rear wheels 11—36 (4-ply)	87 0 0
Twin rear wheels 11—36 (6-ply)	100 0 0
Extended axle and sliding hubs fitted with 14—30 tyres (6-ply)	42 10 0
Extended axle and sliding hubs fitted with 13—30 tyres (6-ply)	33 10 0
Extended axle and sliding hubs fitted with 11—36 tyres (6-ply)	6 10 0
Extended axle and sliding hubs fitted with 11—36 tyres (6-ply)	13 0 0
Extended axle and sliding hubs fitted with 12—36 tyres (6-ply)	29 10 0
All 10/42 Models	
Additional front weight	7 10 0
Radiator shutters and temperature gauge	3 10 0
6·00—16 (6-ply) front tyres in lieu of standard	4 0 0
6·00—19 (6-ply) front tyres in lieu of standard	8 15 0
7·50—16 (6-ply) front tyres in lieu of standard	12 5 0
11—28 (6-ply) rear tyres in lieu of standard	10 10 0
11—32 (6-ply) rear tyres in lieu of standard	22 14 3
13—28 (6-ply) rear tyres in lieu of standard	32 10 9
10—28 (6-ply) Industrial tread tyres in lieu of standard	4 10 0
10—28 (6-ply) Universal tread tyres in lieu of standard	4 10 0
Twin rear wheels 10—28 (4-ply)	60 0 0
Twin rear wheels 11—28 (6-ply)	81 0 0
Heavy Duty clutch	9 2 6

Specification and prices are those obtaining at time of publication; they are liable to alteration without notice

TWELVE MONTHS' WARRANTY   **BACKED BY B.M.C. SERVICE**

10 SPEED GEARBOX
for new 10/42 and 10/60
now you *must* LINK UP WITH
NUFFIELD

A 10-speed gearbox (plus 2 reverse gears) is now standard equipment on both the new 100 m.m. bore 3 and 4 cylinder Nuffield models. Disc-type steering brakes, new instrument panels and numerous detail refinements distinguish these brilliant new tractors on which all these well-known Nuffield features are available:

- ● AUTOMATIC HYDRAULIC DEPTH CONTROL
- ● INDEPENDENT HYDRAULICS (now Dual Flow)
- ● DIFFERENTIAL LOCK
- ● POSITIVELY INDEPENDENT POWER TAKE-OFF

10/42 from £661.10.0   10/60 from £716.10.0

TWELVE MONTHS' WARRANTY and backed by B.M.C. Service   THE **BRITISH** MOTOR CORPORATION LTD

U.254/C

MORRIS MOTORS LTD (Agricultural Sales Division), LONGBRIDGE, BIRMINGHAM.
Overseas business: Nuffield Exports Ltd., Oxford & 41-46 Piccadilly, London, W.1.

PRICE LIST
NUFFIELD
10/42; 10/60 TRACTORS
and
BMC MINI-TRACTOR
APRIL 1966

plus the price tag of £860, would considerably strengthen the competitive position of the Nuffield 10/60, in particular.

However, in one respect he expressed disappointment with the new models and wanted to know why we hadn't done something to change the appearance of the tractor to differentiate it from the old five-speed models?

Frank suggested we paint the wheels white and change the shape of the exhaust. He also went on to express the view that 'all farmers are snobs and they like their neighbours to know as soon as they have something new!' Visually, of course, the tractor had remained virtually unchanged since 1948, but it was now 1964. Looking back, Frank Driffil had a good point, but little did either of us know that within the next three years not only would the wheels of a Nuffield be painted white, but the whole tractor would be given a completely new appearance.

Tipton & Morley of Barnard Castle, Co. Durham were another strong dealer for us and were one of the first Nuffield distributors to be appointed in the north of England. During the time of my association with Tipton & Morley they were a well-run family business headed up by Mr. Tipton senior, and his two sons Peter and Ian. The sales manager was John Atkinson.

One of the very first distributors in Co. Durham, however, was the small family business of Heppell's of Croxdale, who sold a tremendous number of 60hp tractors to industrial users. In due course they were replaced by J. G. Paxton & Sons of Pity Me, who operated the Nuffield franchise alongside that of International Harvester.

Nuffield and IH complemented each other well during the 1960s and 1970s. For this reason, companies such as Platts at Doncaster and Brigg and Rutherfords in south-east Scotland were granted the Nuffield franchise. Nuffield, of course, had the very popular 10/60 and a less competitive smaller tractor; IH's strength, on the other hand, lay in its ability to produce smaller models like the B-414 and 434.

Surprising as it may seem today, almost 50 years on, most ranges from the five British manufacturers were in the same position; each had a big volume seller and a second model that was something of an also ran.

What more can be said about the 10/60 era? White wheels or not, the model was, without doubt, very popular. The sort of job that Val Muir, Brian Webb, Mike Keogh, Martin Stokes and I were doing in the UK was replicated by others in markets around the world. The 10/60 was popular in the Republic of Ireland, in the USA from the east to the west coast, throughout Canada, in Colombia and Venezuela and several other South American countries, South Africa, Kenya, Rhodesia, Australia and New Zealand.

It was sold into most European countries, with the possible exception of Germany, and was particularly successful throughout Scandinavia, with Finland and Denmark being large markets.

But if white wheels were what the market wanted, then white wheels it was going to get! Not just white wheels, but a whole range of major design changes that would completely alter the appearance and technical specification of the Nuffield range, in a way that had not happened for almost 20 years. In 1967 it was time to wave goodbye to the 10/60 and say 'hello' to the 4/65!

Four
Mini
Machinations

It was in late 1963 or early 1964 that, at the request of Tom Cummings, I first visited the headquarters of a company by the name of Tractor Research Ltd, at Toll Bar End, Coventry, where pre-production work on the BMC Mini tractor was centered.

Much security and secrecy surrounded the whole visit; even Tom Cummings didn't reveal its purpose and, as far as I recall, I saw no sign of a tractor while I was there. I had a long discussion with a man called Hubert Higgs, who seemed more keen to learn about me, my background and knowledge of the UK tractor business, than enlightening me as to the purpose of my being there.

This same puzzling experience was shared in turn by colleagues Mike Keogh, Brian Webb and Val Muir. It was only after we made representations to Tom Cummings that a little of the truth began to emerge. Tractor Research had been engaged to develop a new model to supplement the two that, at that time, comprised the Nuffield range.

It is at this stage that my understanding of the politics of the situation differ from some others. For example, I don't believe the Mini tractor was commissioned by BMC. Rather, it is my belief that once the five-year restriction on Harry Ferguson's involvment in tractor development had expired, he launched his company into the development of a new small tractor that he had been persuaded there was a demand for. Ferguson's advisors believed increasing power ratings had left a gap at the bottom end of the market.

I believe the design and development of this new small tractor progressed until, in much the same way as had been the case with the TE-20, it reached a stage at which it was realised they had no means of actually putting it into production themselves. The TE-20 was, of course, produced for Harry Ferguson by the Standard Car Company in Coventry and it was powered by a version of the engine already being used in the large saloon of the time, known as the Standard Vanguard. Having come to this realisation, I believe that a small sales and marketing department was set up, headed by Hubert Higgs. Its aim was to try to sell the design to any one of the then five UK tractor manufacturers who might be interested. It is my contention that only at this stage did BMC, in the guise of Nuffield, become involved.

As far as the engine was concerned, I believe the 948cc diesel engine, based as it was on the petrol engine fitted to the Mini car, was developed specifically for the new Mini tractor with the possibility of it eventually being fitted to a new small car. I say this because it was known that Alec Issigonis, who was in overall charge of all BMC product design and development for the corporation, cherished an ambition to produce the world's smallest, mass-produced, water-cooled diesel engine. The advent of the Mini tractor provided him with the chance to do this.

What I now say is not with the benefit of hindsight. It is a fact that BMC had a perfectly good 1500cc diesel engine already in volume production. Rated at 25hp, it would have met the design criteria laid down by Tractor Research. However, such was his influence that what Issigonis wanted, Issigonis got. What he got on this occasion was the 948cc diesel engine. No matter that some two years later, in a bid to boost sales of the Mini tractor, the 1.5-litre engine was introduced into production, at which stage the BMC Mini designation was replaced by the Nuffield 4/25 (four cylinder/25hp). Tractor Research should, from the outset, have insisted on the existing larger power unit.

TOP:
The Nuffield sales team get to grips with three pre-production Mini tractors at Atherstone. The driving experience was designed to familiarise the sales and service team with the product. Note the tape covering the Mini badge!

LEFT:
A pre-production BMC Mini tractor getting its hands dirty with a MIL front-end loader.

What dare I say about the free linkage draught control system as fitted to the Mini tractor? The subject probably merits a whole article of its own! The staff at Tractor Research went to tremendous lengths to ensure that all Nuffield sales and service personnel were totally familiar with the technicalities of the system. From my experience, I have to say that the operational practicalities were rather more complicated than some have suggested.

Certainly, a very consistent working depth could be achieved for any one of the five possible draught link hitch points, but this consistency was totally dependent upon three consistent factors: soil conditions, forward speed and the weight of the implement.

Also, when using the lowest hitch point to achieve the greatest working depth, the system provided the least amount of weight transfer and, conversely, the highest level of transfer when the hitch point was set to provide minimum operating depth. We soon learnt that the heavier the implement, within reason, the better the linkage performed.

The Ferguson two-furrow plough wasn't as heavy as the Ransomes, which, in turn, was lighter than a two-furrow Bamford (Kverneland). Therefore, we took the latter pair to demonstrations. It was an unfamiliar and unconventional system, but one in which we took a great deal of interest.

As our period of initiation with Tractor Research came to an end, the first supplies of Bathgate-built pre-production Mini tractor prototypes were dispatched to a base we had at Atherstone, just outside Stratford-upon-Avon. It was here, away from the friendly influence of Tractor Research personnel, that we really came to know the new Mini tractor.

Brian Webb, Mike Keogh, Val Muir, Brian Sneyd and myself, together with service colleagues Martin Stokes, Bob Overton, Eric Harris and others, spent many hours figuring out what made the Mini tick and, importantly, how best to demonstrate it to the Nuffield distributor network and the farming public.

By 1965, Nuffield's sales and service teams had spent many, many hours familiarising themselves with the Mini tractor. We had been schooled in its theory and practicalities by the staff at Tractor Research, and had spent several enjoyable days with our own Bathgate-built pre-production tractors at our newly established base at Atherstone.

Nuffield employees Keith Argyle, right, and Brian Webb had plenty to talk about following their BMC Mini tractor ride-and-drive at Atherstone.

TOP:
This Winsam weather frame cab was the height of comfort when the BMC Mini tractor was launched in 1965.
© *British Motor Industry Heritage Trust*

LEFT:
Ron Kettle at the wheel of a 15hp BMC Mini tractor with a MIL front-end loader. The transmission's forward/reverse shuttle arrangement was excellent for this type of work.
© *British Motor Industry Heritage Trust*

TOP:
It took a relaunch,
held in fields in and
around Atherstone,
Warwickshire, to
energise the BMC Mini's
stuttering sales campaign.
© *British Motor Industry
Heritage Trust*

CENTRE:
Forage harvesting wasn't
a typical application for
the 15hp BMC Mini,
but at least two of these
tractor/harvester/trailer
combinations were sold
into the Vale of Evesham.
© *British Motor Industry
Heritage Trust*

RIGHT:
The BMC Mini's
constant mesh gearbox
really came into its own
when used for forward/
reverse applications
such as loading and
buck-raking.
© *British Motor Industry
Heritage Trust*

It's fair to say that we were, without exception, totally enthusiastic about the new BMC Mini. Fitted with a suitable implement there was nothing it wasn't capable of. The 15hp engine would cope with any two-furrow plough we could find (we worked down to 12in and more with a single-furrow reversible Huard or Ferguson plough); we worked down ploughed land at very respectable speeds with disc harrows and other types of cultivator; we sprayed, spread fertiliser, drilled, side-hoed and used the ubiquitous Ferguson three-ton trailer and mounted transport box.

We loaded and moved tons of farmyard manure in all types of confined loose boxes and crew yards, using the new MIL Mini front-end loader. The constant mesh gearbox with its nine forward and three reverse ratios was superb and it really came into its own when used for forward/reverse applications such as loading or buck raking.

Looking back at all this activity, it can probably be said that we were working in isolation, separated almost from the realities of day-to-day farming of the time. Yes, we had a tractor that was doing everything we asked of it, providing it was fitted, as I have already said, with an appropriately sized implement. What perhaps we were blind to was the fact that on the other side of the fence everything was getting bigger; tractors certainly were and new ranges of implements were being introduced to match.

Harry Ferguson's advisers had convinced him there was a gap below these new, larger products, but was it really there? We had all become convinced that it should be. Was the moment of truth very far away?

The launch of the BMC Mini to the distributors and dealers was, by the standards of launches of earlier new Nuffield models, an unusual affair. Arrangements for this, it seemed, had been taken out of the hands of the usual Nuffield staff and it was organised by personnel from the plushly carpeted corridors of car marketing. I don't know for sure, but I suspect it was argued that because this new vehicle was to carry the BMC badge in its model designation, BMC's car marketing department would take care of its launch. How I used to hate tractors being referred to as vehicles.

In any event, the occasion took place in the large, prestigious, circular car show-room at Longbridge, known locally as the Elephant House. Not one single engine was started, not one tractor was driven, and there were no implements. Here, Mr Dealer, is the new BMC Mini tractor; you have seen it, now go out and sell it! Not a good start and certainly not the way it would have been done had Nuffield tractor personnel had their way. A headline from the Daily Express of the time read: 'Mighty little farm hand drives in'.

The piece, written by Alexander Kenworthy, went on to say: "A miniature farm tractor which will add power to the elbows of millions of small farmers is launched by Britain on to a vast world market today. It is the British Motor Corporation's agricultural version of the mini-car – a farmyard runabout which can cope with most of the field tasks performed by its big brothers."

Mr Alexander went on to say: "The manufacturers have spent £5mn developing the mini-tractor in the past six years. Its power unit is a new 15hp diesel engine of 948cc based on the petrol engine already used in two million cars. This four-cylinder water-cooled 'mighty atom' is claimed by BMC to be the smallest mass-produced diesel made in Britain. Just over 8ft long and 3ft 8in high, the farm mini costs a basic

£512 and £585 with hydraulics and lights. It will also be an economical second tractor on big farms for farmyard tasks and light field work. It is designed as an all-purpose machine which will do all the tasks required on about 100,000 small farms in Britain and millions in other parts of the world."

He also added that: "BMC anticipate big sales in developing countries such as India, who urgently need tractor power to boost food output."

The mighty atom power unit was indeed the smallest, mass-produced, water-cooled diesel engine manufactured in Britain, and almost certainly the world at that time. The brain-child of Alec Issigonis, it was a super little engine for its horsepower. Sadly, the early versions were not good at starting from cold and this necessitated a huge 67Ah battery, which was nearly as big as the engine itself! Later versions of the same engine were fitted with modified glow-plug heating systems, which helped, but the problem was never overcome completely.

It has to be said that the launch was not the success it should have been. Orders did not flow in and tractors coming off the Bathgate production line exceeded demand almost from day one. There was an element of incredulity on the part of many distributors. Yes, they had wanted a lighter, more manoeuvrable mid-range tractor than the three-cylinder 10/42, something that would compete more effectively with the Massey Ferguson 35, Fordson Dexta and similar sized models from IH and David Brown, but they considered this new tractor as Mini by name, and by nature.

Many dealers were disinclined to give it a second thought at this early stage. A few dealers saw the Mini in a different light. These included J. W. Glover at Warwick (under the leadership of John Martin), some of the other branches of the F. H. Burgess Group, Appleyard of Wetherby and a little later, T. Parker & Sons at Worcester Park. They all identified a niche in the market in their localities, and targeted their sales and demonstration activities in that specific direction with not inconsiderable success.

BELOW LEFT:
Here I am putting the Nuffield 4/35 through its paces during a working demonstration in Warwickshire in mid-1968. The Nuffield 4/25 used a new 1.5-litre BMC diesel engine.
© *British Motor Industry Heritage Trust*

BELOW RIGHT:
Front wheel weights, a full complement of front weights and a loader help to keep the front end down on this Nuffield 4/25 fitted with a Sanderson rear forklift.
© *British Motor Industry Heritage Trust*

Overall, however, volumes remained small and far from sufficient to sustain the flow of units being pumped out by Bathgate.

A relaunch was planned and staged on land in and around Atherstone. It was planned that a fleet of Minis would be shown performing every conceivable task, whether the season would normally allow this or not. Kale was drilled with a four-row drill so that side-hoeing could be demonstrated; potatoes were planted and then harvested with a spinner; we rotavated with a 40in Howard; and straw was baled with a small Bamfords baler. There was even a forage harvester and three-ton trailer combination. As a matter of interest, Glovers at Warwick subsequently sold two of these combinations into the Vale of Evesham for harvesting parsley.

We had a McConnel ditcher, an Atlas Copco compressor and pneumatic drill, ploughs, cultivators, an electricity generator, everything and anything that the Mini and its 15hp would handle.

This relaunch went on for two full weeks. We had daily groups of distributors and dealers, journalists from publications as diverse as the Farmers Weekly, Farmer & Stockbreeder and the Financial Times, plus representatives from national and local government, ADAS, local authorities, industrial users, golf courses, cricket grounds and implement manufacturers.

Needless to say, everybody was well fed and watered in a huge marquee in one of the fields; I seem to recall that steak and kidney pie was a popular choice! A 16mm film had been produced entitled 'Seeing is Believing' and this was shown following lunch every day. As a result of all this promotional activity, plus follow-up demonstrations and an on-going advertising campaign, sales of the Mini did begin to improve. A new member of staff, Stan Whittingham-Jones, was given a roving commission to specialise in non-agricultural markets such as local authorities, turf maintenance and light industrial applications.

Stan was indeed a specialist and he introduced us to the need for turf tyres and dual rear wheels. He was a competent demonstrator and was responsible for the sale of many Minis into this sector of the market, at a time when the likes of Kubota and Iseki were unknown in this country.

However, with as little as 15hp under the bonnet the Mini continued to be difficult to sell. After only two years in production, what should have been done from day one eventually happened. The existing, proven, easy-starting 1.5-litre BMC diesel engine (rated at 25hp) was fitted in production at Bathgate. Sadly, in some ways, the engine it replaced was allowed to disappear into oblivion. At the same time the tractor was redesignated as the Nuffield 4/25 (four-cylinder/25hp). With an additional 10hp, and good ones at that, this model and the Leyland 154 which came later proved to be a much more valuable addition to the Nuffield range.

A latter day commentator once wrote that sales were always disappointing, adding that perhaps the story would have been different if Harry Ferguson, super salesman that he had been, had lived to guide his company's last project through to fruition. Well, I don't think so. As an engineering exercise the tractor was excellent, but it was at least one decade too late in coming to the market, irrespective of which part of the world it was sold.

Examples of the sales material produced for the BMC Mini tractor. Note how there was no reference to Nuffield on any of the Mini tractor brochures. © British Motor Industry Heritage Trust

In the UK, higher horsepower units were already superseding the TE-20 and its counterparts. Rightly or wrongly, farmers world-wide were demanding more and more horsepower and sophistication. When we look at what's being sold today, that trend is still continuing.

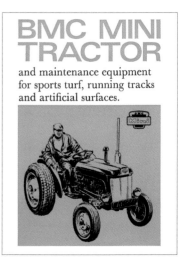

Five
Not Such a
Great Improvement

When Nuffield introduced the 4/25 (four-cylinder/25hp) in 1967 it was a logical and much-needed improvement on the under-powered BMC Mini. While the new 1.5-litre engine didn't exactly transform the 4/25, it did make a huge difference to its overall performance.

What was not generally known at this time, certainly not by myself and my colleagues, was that the introduction of the Mini tractor and its successors was not the end of the association between Tractor Research Limited and BMC's agricultural division.

At some point in 1967 Tom Cummings called a sales meeting in his office at Longbridge to announce that our two largest models, the 10/42 and 10/60, were to be replaced later in the year.

The same team responsible for the Mini tractor had carried out all the design work for the new tractors. Previously this work had been the responsibility of the Tractor & Transmissions division in Birmingham.

As well as they continued to perform in fields right across the world, the fundamental design of the 10/42 and 10/60 tractors was essentially unchanged from that originally put on the drawing board some 20 years previously. Perhaps it had been accepted in the corridors of power, those remote parts of the huge Longbridge complex where ordinary mortals rarely ventured, that some more elementary design changes were now the order of the day.

This tumultuous decision would almost certainly have been taken at the highest level, probably by the then chairman of the Corporation, Sir George Harriman, and his engineering director, Alec Issigonis. They in turn instructed Tractor Research Limited, the company responsible for the Mini tractor, to work on the designs for the next generation of Nuffield tractors.

It has to be said that in spite of excellent sales around the world and very competitive levels of performance, the 10/42 and 10/60 were becoming dated in terms of their appearance and general design. The competition was moving on, with Ford, who introduced its all-new 6X series in 1964, leading the way.

Most importantly though, positive decisions were being taken about the future of the Nuffield range. As a result, the 3/45 and 4/65 tractors were introduced in 1967. All the detailed design work on these two models had been carried out for BMC by Tractor Research Limited. To this day I do not know who drew up the design brief, but it was wide ranging, going much further than the redesignated model numbers and increase in power to 45hp and 65hp.

Space does not allow me to detail every single one of the changes – there were so many. Compared with previous four-cylinder Nuffields, the 4/65's wheelbase was increased by 8in. This was achieved by lengthening the main frame, providing not only an improvement in front-end stability, but also considerably better access to the driver's platform. The driving area became far less cluttered and more spacious.

For better or for worse (some would say the latter, with the benefit of hindsight), a redesigned fuel tank was mounted vertically forward of the radiator, and a new instrument panel incorporating, probably for the first time on any tractor, printed circuitry, was mounted forward of the steering wheel.

The wheel itself was smaller than usual and, as a sop to the stylists, it was white! So it was that one of the unique features of the original Nuffield design, the offset steering wheel, was consigned to history.

Another item that went the same way was the huge front-end weight, all 270lb (122.5kg) of it. Once fitted, this front-end weight was rarely removed. It was replaced by a set of eight hook-on hand weights which, taking into account their forward mounting, provided an additional axle load of around 700lb. Furthermore, they were much easier to take on and off.

The hydraulic system was re-engineered and for the first time Nuffield tractors featured a double-acting top link and a proper hydraulic quadrant, although it was still felt that position control wasn't necessary.

A Nuffield 4/65 prepares the ground at Coleshill ahead of the official dealer/press launch in 1967.

A new power steering arrangement, driven direct from the engine timing gears, as opposed to the earlier belt-driven design, was introduced. Incredible as it may seem today, this was still available only as a factory fitted option, incurring an extra cost of £65 to the customer.

All these changes and many more were universally welcomed when they were revealed to UK and export personnel. As for the new styling, let's just say it didn't go down too well with some members of the team! As far as I remember, the 3/45 and 4/65 were styled by designers at Longbridge, not by Tractor Research.

We now had white wheels and wide, practical mudguards, but we also had a new bonnet line that was so very different from the purposeful, workmanlike Nuffield outline recognised throughout the world. Needless to say, it took some members of the sales team quite some time to come to terms with the appearance of these two new models.

For better or for worse, the new designs were, as the saying goes, cast in stone. We set about planning the all-important introductions to the distributor and dealer networks and, of course, to the gentlemen of the agricultural press. Jack Green's farm at Coleshill near Sutton Coldfield was chosen as the venue for the event, which unlike the earlier Mini launch was a full working demonstration.

In the field, the 3/45 (three-cylinder/45hp) proved to be a worthy successor to earlier three-cylinder Nuffields; it performed extremely well with a Ransomes TS83 (three furrow x 12in reversible). Brian Webb, who was always a fan of Ransomes products, made sure that it starred on equal terms with anything we could put behind the 4/65, so much so that he is immortalised on the front cover of one of the 3/45 brochures driving this exact combination.

What a super power unit that long-stroke BMC three-cylinder engine was; spinning at 1350rpm, its 127lb ft torque was considerably better than any other equivalent powered competitor.

Strange as it may seem today, John Deere was only just beginning to launch its own small tractors in the UK. Perhaps Deere will forgive me if I remind them of the

BELOW LEFT:
The Nuffield 4/65's pulling power, or torque, put it ahead of many rivals, including Deere. It was good at pushing, too and could be equipped with a dozer blade.
© British Motor Industry Heritage Trust

BELOW RIGHT:
A new instrument panel, incorporating printed circuitry, was mounted forward of the steering wheel on the Nuffield 3/45 and 4/65 tractors introduced in 1967.

inadequacies of its 1020 which, at 47hp, could muster only 109lb ft of torque at 1500rpm. The company's 1120, at 52hp, managed just 118.6lb ft spinning at the same speed.

Deere, together with Ford, Fiat and one or two others, had opted for short stroke, over-square engines. But then perhaps I should also acknowledge that he who laughs last, laughs longest.

So I still have fond memories of the Nuffield 3/45's excellent three-cylinder BMC engine and its quite exceptional torque characteristics. The four-cylinder version of the same engine that went into the new 4/65 shared the same bore/stroke ratio and was, therefore, also a long-stroke power unit. Developing 65hp, hence the model designation 4/65, it produced a very good flat torque curve peaking at 170lb ft at 1350rpm. However, this figure didn't give it the same sort of torque leadership as its three-cylinder brother.

TOP:
The Nuffield 4/65, seen here with a Bamfords five-furrow semi-mounted plough at the 1967 National Ploughing Championships, was a distinct departure from the 10/60.

RIGHT:
Performance characteristics for the Nuffield 3/45 and 4/65 were contained in this 'Power' booklet, published in 1967.
© *British Motor Industry Heritage Trust*

For example, the more powerful Massey Ferguson 178, Ford 5000 and David Brown 1200 did produce better figures on paper, but in the case of the latter, at much higher, fuel-slurping revs. Market leaders in terms of engine efficiency were undoubtedly International's B-450 and 634. Not only did they have quite exceptional maximum torque figures of 200lb ft and 225lb ft respectively, they achieved these figures with their engines spinning at only 1100rpm and 1200rpm. For some reason, however, they were never big-volume sellers.

Bottom of this particular class once again was John Deere with its 2020 and 2120, whose over-square engines could only claim relatively low max torque figures at 1500rpm. No doubt somebody could tell me why it was that Ford's over-square engines could claim max torque figures as far down the speed range as they did?

From the point of view of overall performance, those of us who were involved with selling and servicing Nuffields firmly believed that tractors with long-stroke, slow-revving engines were better products. Out in the field we rarely had a problem in proving this to be the case.

Returning for a little while to Jack Green's farm at Coleshill, and the distributor and dealer launch of the 3/45 and 4/65, I was reminded recently of one dealer principal, who should, perhaps, remain nameless. After watching Brian Webb on the 3/45 ploughing with the Ransomes TS83 three furrow x 12in reversible plough he commented that he was "only scratching the surface".

Brian, in his own inimitable way, responded that of course he was – it was the whole point of the exercise! By this he meant that he was showing off the capability of the new hydraulics. The new double-acting top link allowed the operator to plough or cultivate at minimum depths, something that previous Nuffield hydraulic systems had difficulty doing with any degree of consistency. It was an area that dealers and farmers had rightly complained about ever since the introduction of the first Nuffield draft control system on the 342 and 460.

The field launch of our two new 3/45 and 4/65 models lasted for several days and was well planned and executed. As always, it was a good team effort, with colleagues such as Brain Webb, Brian Sneyd, Val Muir, Mike Keogh, Martin Stokes and several others all playing their respective parts. The field demonstration also included a Bray 4/65, which replaced the earlier 10/60 version.

The Bray was a four-wheel drive conversion with equal wheels all round. The company's demonstrator, Fred, a young man with a bushy brown beard, was one of those characters who could keep the workforce amused all day with stories and songs, some repeatable and some not! Fred Bray, as we knew him, spent a lot of time with the Nuffield demonstration team as it toured the country following the public launch of the new models.

The Bray versions of the Nuffield and later Leyland sold particularly well in certain export markets, notably for heavy haulage work in sugar cane plantations.

Also contributing to the overall success of the launch were personnel from Tractor Research at nearby Coventry, where the two new models had been developed. Colleagues from the various implement manufacturers, whose products we were demonstrating with the tractors, were also present, as they always were.

Implements made by Bamfords of Uttoxeter always played a big part at Nuffield events, and in this respect we had area sales manager Chris Banbury and service manager Cyril Dyke present on one of the days. Cyril was well known throughout the agricultural machinery business and I seem to recall that at a later stage in his career with Bamfords he became involved in a sales and marketing capacity.

Around the time of the launch of the 3/45 and 4/65, Bamfords lost the import rights for a particular make of forage harvester. Not long afterwards they introduced a replacement, one of their own designs which they manufactured in-house. The national advertising for this carried a working photograph of the large red machine, below which a caption read 'Bamfords have got a big chopper'. Cyril Dyke was credited with this bit of original copy writing!

Happily, the entire agricultural machinery business, whether manufacturing or retailing, was liberally sprinkled with characters with whom it became a pleasure to work. On the retail side there was a minority who were never prepared to see the brighter and lighter side of working life. In the main, though, each day was made enjoyable by the quality and nature of the people with whom the business had to be done.

Take, for example, the Nuffield distributorship in Carmarthen, a large and successful family business owned and run by the Lowndes family. Trading as Lowndes Garages Ltd, they held all the franchises on the Morris side of BMC, including the famous car marques of Morris, Wolseley, Riley, Vanden Plas and MG, together with Morris Commercials. Their Nuffield franchise operated from completely separate premises on Richmond Terrace, Carmarthen.

The tractor side of the business was managed by Michael Lowndes, with David Agget as his sales manager. It is no exaggeration to say that Michael, David and the whole of their staff, whether in the workshop, parts department, administration or driving the delivery lorry were completely dedicated to the Nuffield tractor. To conduct your business in such an environment was never an onerous task. David Agget sold hundreds of three- and four-cylinder tractors throughout Carmarthenshire and Pembrokeshire, and doubtless many of those tractors will still be around on farms today.

Lowndes Garages were not alone in their dedication to Nuffield: there were many distributors up and down the country of the same calibre, and I will mention some more of these later in my story.

But back to the 3/45 and 4/65 and their public launch in 1967. The Nuffield team was by now totally trained up on all the new features, we were familiar with all the facts and figures of the new specifications, and we had had a useful amount of field experience with them. We were ready to meet our customers and sell them the characteristics and benefits of the new models.

But what about pricing? It was with incredulity that we learnt that the 4/65 was to be the first tractor in the country to have a price tag of over £1000. Had there been a printing error in the price list? Could a tractor priced at £1059.00 actually be sold? Of course it could, but it just shows how times and prices have changed more than a little since then.

Not long after the launch of the 3/45 and 4/65 models, problems began to appear. How, after a product planning programme lasting several years, involving both prototype and pre-production testing, both on test rigs and in the field, could a new tractor

TOP:
Nuffield's 3/45 and 4/65 field launch was a prestigious affair, taking place over several days at Coleshill, near Sutton Coldfield.

CENTRE:
When launched in 1967, the Nuffield 4/65 was the first tractor in the country to have a price tag of over £1000. It seemed like a lot of money in those days!

LEFT:
The new Nuffield 4/65 developed 65hp at 2200rpm. Its main rivals at the time were the MF 178, Ford 5000 and DB 1200.

range be introduced into the marketplace and immediately run into fairly major and glaringly obvious technical problems?

It would probably be wrong of me to mention problems of this nature experienced by other manufacturers, even though most of them have, at some time or other, run into a catalogue of errors immediately after the launch of new models. In the case of the Nuffield 4/65 there were two major problems that became apparent from the first day we put the launch tractors in to Jack Green's fields at Coleshill.

The first was a high-frequency vibration that was felt throughout the whole of the tractor. The driver felt these vibrations as he rested his feet on the foot-boards, through his hands on the steering wheel, and through his posterior on the newly designed

RIGHT:
Later MkII versions of the Nuffield 4/65 were identified by a silver bonnet stripe. This one is equipped with 15 x 30 wheels, front wheel weights and a Hydrovane compressor.
© *British Motor Industry Heritage Trust*

BELOW LEFT:
Looking every bit a dedicated loading shovel, a Nuffield 4/65 equipped with 14 x 30 rears, Tractor Vision cab and Mil Master front-end loader.
© *British Motor Industry Heritage Trust*

BELOW RIGHT:
A 1968 Nuffield 4/65 MkII finds itself engaged on refuse site duties, equipped with a Winsam cab, dual wheels and a Wheatley trailer.
© *British Motor Industry Heritage Trust*

sprung seat. It was evident as you looked at the needles of the various dials on the smart new instrument panel, and even more of a problem when the bonnet badges and other such items began to drop off!

The second problem, insufficient cooling capacity, was an elementary design flaw. Just how could a team of experienced design engineers allow a tractor to go forward into production with such a basic shortcoming?

If a group of sales and service personnel such as ourselves were able to experience the problem within a day or so of putting the tractors to work in average north Warwickshire field conditions, how on earth did a team of field test engineers not notice the same problem? They spent months and probably years carrying out their development work in fields not a million miles away in south Warwickshire and Gloucestershire. Nearly 50 years on and words still fail me.

Perhaps the new fuel tank, mounted forward of the radiator, wasn't such a good idea after all? And those smart poly 'V' pulleys and matching fan belt also soon lost both their technical and novelty value; try as they might they couldn't drive the cooling fan with sufficient efficiency to pull enough air through the radiator.

At a stroke, the 4/65 introduced two major problems that its predecessors had never experienced – faults that kept Bob Overton, Eric Harris and Martin Stokes, Nuffield's very competent UK service engineers of the time, at full stretch for many, many months. Eventually, with the introduction of several design changes, the cooling problem was brought under control. Vibration, a problem never encountered with the faithful BMC 38TD diesel engine, continued to cause trouble until the introduction of the harmonic crankshaft balancer in early 1969. But by then the damage had already been done.

By Nuffield standards, the 3/45 and 4/65 had a comparatively short production run of three years. Midway through this, in May 1968, the British Motor Corporation was merged with the Leyland Motor Corporation to form the British Leyland Motor Corporation (BLMC). Sir George Harriman, the ex-apprentice who rose through the ranks to become the long-serving chairman of BMC, stood down at this time and Lord Stokes of Leyland became chairman and managing director of the new giant conglomerate. And gigantic it certainly was.

Earlier in my story I touched upon the somewhat parlous state of today's manufacturing and engineering capacity in this country, and the effect this is having on the availability of real jobs and employment. Almost from day one, BLMC was exporting vehicles to the value of over £1mn every working day. Based on turnover, the company ranked as the second largest vehicle producer in Europe and the fifth largest in the world, with sales totalling over £900mn per annum.

In spite of this manufacturing strength, those of us in the Nuffield tractor division were more than a little concerned about our future. It was known by some that Lord Stokes had at some time in the not too distant past already killed off Standard's tractor development programme.

History here is a little difficult to relate because of the complexities of various mergers and take-overs, but it is all pertinent to the history of the Nuffield tractor and the part played in it by myself, my colleagues and Lord Stokes himself, so bear with me while I try to explain.

The Leyland Motor Corporation, the new partner in this conglomerate, had taken over the Standard-Triumph Group in 1961. Standard-Triumph had many claims to fame, among which can be numbered such cars as the Triumph Herald and, some years before that, the Standard Vanguard. A version of the Vanguard engine was fitted in Harry Ferguson's TE range of tractors. More than that, it was during the Vanguard era that the Standard Motor Company actually produced the TE range of tractors for Harry Ferguson in Coventry.

The arrangement between Ferguson and Standard continued until the Ferguson company became part of Massey-Harris, at which time Standard lost the rights to the production of the grey Fergie. This had, of course, been an important part of their business. Faced with the prospect of an empty production facility, they set about designing and developing their own replacement.

The new V-pulley and fan belt used on the Nuffield 4/65 couldn't drive the cooling fan with sufficient efficiency to pull enough air through the radiator.

Standard built a number of prototype tractors and field-tested them prior to and during 1961, at which time Donald Stokes and his Leyland Motors company not only acquired Standard-Triumph, but sadly also cancelled the tractor programme. Those of us who have seen one of the remaining tractors would say what a huge mistake this probably was. Standard's tractor, while somewhat larger than the TE-20, was powered by the same Standard engine as the grey Ferguson. However, its specifications (clutch, transmission, brakes, hydraulics and PTO) would not look out of place in technical data sheets of a much later era and for its time it was a very up to date tractor.

It is thought that four prototypes have survived. One of the tractors was taken up to the Leyland tractor factory at Bathgate by Ralph Wiggington, on his appointment as tractor design manager for the firm. Ralph had worked on the design of the Standard tractor at Banner Lane. When the Leyland business was sold to Marshall in 1981 the Standard tractor was taken to a garage in the south-west of Scotland by Leyland's engineering director, Bob Beresford, who refurbished it prior to delivering it to Gainsborough.

It was put on display alongside other Nuffield, Leyland and Marshall exhibits in the newly created museum. When Marshall succumbed to economic pressures in 1985, the Standard was moved to Scunthorpe. It now resides in a superb collection of vintage tractors owned by former Marshall dealer, Robert Crawford of Frithville, Boston.

Robert's tractor may have been the last prototype to be produced because, unlike other survivors, it has styling that distinguishes it from that of a Ferguson TE-20. I believe it has what was planned to be the final transmission design that incorporated a forward and reverse shuttle.

Michael Thorne has a complete prototype Standard tractor in his collection in Devon together with parts of another and he believes that a fourth exists somewhere in the Midlands.

BELOW LEFT:
Michael Thorne's prototype Standard tractor is one of only four known survivors.

BELOW RIGHT:
What is believed to be a late prototype of the Standard tractor, pictured when it was part of the Marshall museum at Gainsborough during the mid-1980s.

Despite the uncertainties surrounding the creation of BLMC, we were a team of enthusiastic people dedicated to the Nuffield tractor, with a new chairman and managing director who less than a decade earlier had cancelled what appeared to be a very promising new tractor programme when it was at an advanced stage of development. What did the future hold for us, and for our beloved Nuffield tractor, with this new man at the helm?

In the event, it didn't take long for some of our concerns to be eased. Tom Cummings and Mike Warland were still in overall charge of UK sales, working from their Longbridge office. Not long after the formation of British Leyland, we were informed of the appointment of a new man, Bob Turner, whose title of tractor sales director was a new one at Nuffield. Bob Turner had previously been with Ford Motor Company's tractor division and it appeared that he had been head-hunted on the instructions of Lord Stokes.

The termination of the arrangement with Tractor Research at Coventry was the second major change that took place following the formation of British Leyland. It seemed that the new board of directors did not want the development of their products to be in the hands of an outside operation.

Details of a new, in-house tractor development department began to emerge, one that would be based up at Bathgate in Scotland. It would be under the management of Ralph Wiggington. Although it was not known to us at this time, it later emerged that Ralph Wiggington had played a fairly major role in the development of the Standard tractor at Coventry, the one that was killed off by our new chairman.

So, we had a new sales director and were going to have a new design department. Perhaps Lord Stokes wasn't such a bad sort after all. Perhaps the future of the Nuffield tractor would now be more secure?

As part of its marketing campaign for the 3/45 and 4/65 models, Nuffield sent out the 'Two New Tractors' brochure, *left*, as a magazine insert and also produced a lavish 16-page sales brochure, *right*, for general distribution.

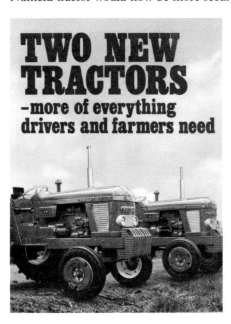

Six

New Name,
New Colour

Isn't it strange how the most important and serious business events can often have a humorous and light-hearted side to them? The arrival of Bob Turner as Nuffield Tractors' sales director from Ford was, in the early days following the formation of British Leyland, extremely important to the shape of the business.

Some months before Bob's arrival on the scene, the export sales division had appointed a new member of staff to represent the company and promote the sales of Nuffield tractors throughout South America.

This was James H. Taylor (known to some as James H and to others simply as Jim). He, too, had made the move across from the Ford tractor operation, where he had been one of their most respected demonstrators. At some stage he had worked for Bob Turner.

On his arrival at Nuffield, James Taylor let it be known that one of his main reasons for leaving Ford was to get away from Bob Turner who, to put it mildly, he described as being something of a task master. It wasn't that James was afraid of hard work, far from it.

But just imagine his surprise on returning from a lengthy trip to his South American territory (knowing Jim, with a briefcase full of orders) to find that his old boss at Ford was now his new boss at Nuffield! In spite of this, Jim played a long and significant part in the history of Nuffield and Leyland tractors, not just in export markets but in the UK as well.

Ordinary mortals such as myself were never privy to the detailed briefs that Bob Turner was given from senior management, unless it directly affected us in the course of our work. One of the first changes he brought about was to relocate both the home and export sales offices from Longbridge to Bathgate, a move that took place in late 1967 or early 1968. This involved personnel such as Tom Cummings, Mike Warland and Ron Kettle, along with Bob himself, moving north to Scotland. This was an eminently sensible move in many ways, not least because it helped in the development of closer working relationships with people whose job it was to turn paper orders into real tractors.

The second really major change was revealed to sales and service personnel in the autumn of 1969, when we were informed of the first radical changes to the tractor range. Incredibly, or so it seemed at the time, the Nuffield name was to be dropped, with all future tractor models to be known as Leyland.

The rationale behind this thinking was that while Nuffield was a well known and respected name in certain overseas markets, there were many countries that had not yet been developed. It was argued that in these potential new markets, and in all others, Leyland was a recognised household name, whereas Nuffield wasn't.

Furthermore, the tractors were to be restyled. Nobody really regretted this change as the appearance of the Nuffield 3/45 and 4/65 was far from popular. Of more immediate concern was the loss of the much-loved orange colour scheme that was so closely associated with Nuffield.

The new Leyland tractors were to be painted a two-tone blue with silver wheels. Was this, we wondered, a hangover from Bob Turner's time at Ford? Was it, perhaps, an attempt to capitalise on the colour of one of the world's best-selling ranges of tractors? We were informed in no uncertain terms that neither was the case: the change to the blue colour scheme had been decided upon simply because that combination of colours was the house colour of the new company, British Leyland.

To many of us in the sales and service departments at the time, the saddest aspect of the changes taking place was the demise of the three-cylinder version of the BMC engine used in the 3/45. What a superb performer this 2.8-litre engine had been. Nevertheless, the powers that be argued that it was too costly to produce in the relatively low volumes in which it was required for tractor production, even though many of its components were common to its four-cylinder counterpart! Latterly I came to learn that the management at the Bathgate factory, laid out as it was for massive volume production, were no fans of manufacturing complexity. The three-cylinder engine was cancelled to reduce complexity on the engine production line and to reduce manufacturing costs.

The Leyland range of tractors was, therefore, to consist initially of three models: the 70hp 384 (3.8-litre, 4-cylinder), the 55hp 344 (3.4-litre, 4-cylinder) and the 25hp 154 (1.5-litre, 4-cylinder). Under the stage management of Bob Turner, a major launch to both the agricultural press and to the distributors and dealers took place at a conference centre at Alexandra Palace.

This was our first experience of Bob as an organiser of this type of theatre-based launch the like of which we had never seen at Nuffield before. An element of surprise was always high on Bob's list of priorities, and on this occasion it was achieved when Stan Whittingham-Jones drove a 154 through an imitation brick wall on to an empty stage!

However, despite Stan's indisputable talent for demonstrating the 154 and its Mini and 4/25 predecessors on the wide open spaces of golf courses and cricket fields, he incurred the wrath of Bob Turner on this occasion. He managed to do this by grating the gears of the 154 as he prepared to drive it through the wall, thereby alerting the audience to the fact that there were tractors hidden behind it, which rather ruined Bob's intended surprise!

TOP:
This publicity photograph from the time of the introduction of the Leyland tractor brand and colour scheme in 1969 shows a 154 (25hp) loading a 384 (70hp).
© *British Motor Industry Heritage Trust*

CENTRE:
As part of the final pre-production testing, a Leyland 344 and 384 carried out a 10-day, non-stop ploughing marathon from 20-30 October 1969. They ploughed a total of 830 acres. The team involved consisted of, from left, Tony Lamm, Vincent de las Casas, Ron Kettle, Tony Higgs, Brian Sneyd, Brian Webb, Doug Mitchell, John Arkell, Aiden Kendall, John Handbury, Martin Taylor and Bob Twaddle.
© *British Motor Industry Heritage Trust*

LEFT:
No wonder I'm smiling, left, because one of the dealers under my wing, Robert B. Massey of Market Weighton, had just taken out nine Ford tractors, replacing them with Leyland 344s and 384s. Dealer principal Robert Massey, third from left, congratulates the new owner on his purchase.
© *British Motor Industry Heritage Trust*

RIGHT:
Leyland demonstrator
Ray Runciman holds aloft
the Suffolk Farm Machinery
Club's trophy, won for the
'Best Ploughing in the
British Ploughing Match
Demonstrations'. Joining him
were fellow demonstrators
Ian Jack, left, and George
Livingstone.
© *British Motor Industry
Heritage Trust*

CENTRE:
Introduced in 1971, the
Leyland 253 was the first
model in the range to use
the three-cylinder Perkins
3.152 engine rated at 47hp.
This one was being used on
grass tyres for pulling gang
mowers on a golf course on
the outskirts of London.
© *British Motor Industry
Heritage Trust*

BELOW LEFT:
Apart from cosmetic
alterations, Leyland's new
154 was essentially the
same as its predecessor,
the 25hp Nuffield 4/25.
© *British Motor Industry
Heritage Trust*

BELOW RIGHT:
A rear view of the Leyland
safety cab with its flexible
rear window rolled up. Also
shown is the factory-fitted
pick-up hitch supplied by
ARM of Staffordshire.
© *British Motor Industry
Heritage Trust*

The 154 was followed by the 344 and 384, revealing for the very first time the far-reaching changes that had been made to accompany the introduction of the name 'Leyland'. This press and trade launch was followed in December 1969 by the first public showing of the new range at the Royal Smithfield Show.

I remember that particular Smithfield Show being busy, very busy. The same applied to the Royal Show of 1970 and also to the Smithfield of that year. Public reaction to the new blue Leyland range was proving very positive, both at home and abroad, and production volumes at Bathgate were increased on a progressive basis in an effort to keep pace with the demand.

At the Smithfield Show of 1971 we launched the 47hp Leyland 253 (2.5-litre, 3-cylinder), a replacement in many respects for the old Nuffield 3/45. With the arrival of the 253 we were once more able to cross swords with the MF 135 and Ford 3000. Furthermore, the 253 shared its three-cylinder Perkins 3.152 engine, or at least a very similar version, with the popular Massey Ferguson 135.

At this same time all our show tractors were exhibited with a new safety cab, one which was designed to comply with legislation to meet crush and impact test requirements, thereby protecting the driver in the event of an overturn. Whilst such cabs on all makes of tractor were, no doubt, an invaluable safety aid, they took no account of the noise problem. As a result, drivers on most makes of tractor in the early 1970s found themselves sitting in nothing better than a sound amplification box.

With the new Perkins-engined Leyland 253 we were able to demonstrate how the weight and transmission of a tractor could affect its overall performance. The 253 with, for all practical purposes, the same engine as the MF 135, could out-perform it when it came to heavier-duty draft work. And in common with its three-cylinder Nuffield predecessors, the Leyland 253 was a much more sure-footed tractor on hill-sides and steep going.

The demand for tractors of this size was steadily declining, though, as farmers began to ask for tractors with more horsepower. How would Leyland meet this demand? In house, thoughts had already begun to focus on a well-proven engine with not three, but six cylinders. The resulting 285, 2100, 485 and 4100 models were a step in the right direction, but by no means perfect, as we'll discover later.

BRITISH LEYLAND FAMILY TREE

BRITISH MOTOR HOLDINGS	LEYLAND MOTOR CORPORATION
1905 – Austin Motor Company Ltd	1896 – Steam Motor Company
1913 – W. R. M. Motors Ltd	1907 – Leyland Motors
1922 – Hotchkiss Company	1919 – Leyland Motors Ltd
1923 – Morris Commercial Cars Ltd	1945 – West Yorkshire Foundries Ltd
1926 – Morris Motors Ltd	1951 – Albion Motors Ltd
1927 – Wolseley Motors Ltd	1955 – Scammell Lorries Ltd
1938 – Riley (Coventry) Ltd	1960 – Self-Changing Gears Ltd
1952 – The British Motor Corporation Ltd	1961 – Standard-Triumph Group
1953 – Fisher & Ludlow Ltd	1962 – Assoc. Commercial Vehicles
1966 – British Motor Holdings formed	1963 – Leyland Motor Corp. founded
1967 – Jaguar Cars Ltd	1967 – Rover Group
1968 – Aveling-Barford Group	1968 – British Leyland

With the arrival of Bob Turner at Leyland, greater emphasis was placed on publicity and promotion. Probably because of the time he spent with the Ford Tractors operation, Bob was much more switched on about this aspect of marketing.

As an example of this, a really excellent 16mm film was produced to support the launch of the new Leyland tractor range. This purported to show the very final stages of the pre-production testing of the new models. The film covered a ten-day, non-stop ploughing marathon using Leyland 344 and 384 tractors and Bamfords (Kverneland) ploughs on farms spread across the Mid- and East Lothians.

It was a truly non-stop exercise, the two tractors being driven by teams of drivers night and day, and refuelled on the move from a mobile bowser pulled by a Leyland 154. Records were kept of fuel consumption and acres ploughed, and reference to the performance figures was made in the accompanying commentary.

Some copies of this film still exist, as they do of another one made in the early 1970s, entitled 'Crossing Frontiers'. This was particularly interesting for the operational variations it showed of the 344 and 384 tractors working in many of the export markets right across the world, from snow ploughing in the depths of a Finnish winter to spraying citrus groves in the heat of a South African summer.

These two films, together with the later ones that were used to promote the introduction of the Synchro transmission and the four-wheel drive 462 and 472 models (more on both of these developments a little further on), proved to be excellent promotional tools. They were costly to produce, being made at a time when camcorders and the like were probably never even on designers' drawing boards. But they were good value for money and formed the basis of many interesting evenings with machinery clubs, Young Farmers Clubs and agricultural colleges.

Not long after the introduction of the new Leylands in late 1969, another promotional opportunity presented itself to tractor manufacturers – the Long Sutton Tractor Trials, held in south Lincolnshire and organised by the Long Sutton & District Agricultural Society.

Being based up north in Bathgate, the Leyland demonstration unit didn't perhaps fully appreciate the significance of this event. Our subsequent participation was left in the hands of the local distributor, Levertons of Spalding, who entered one of the new 384s together with a three-furrow reversible plough.

The aim of the Long Sutton Tractor Trials was to measure the performance of the tractors entered. The results were collated on a chart so that the farming public could compare the performance of each tractor.

To put things into perspective, the performance figures for the 384 weren't very good; in fact, in terms of recorded wheel-slip and acres ploughed per hour, they were the worst of the lot. The first I heard about this was when I received an internal memo from Bob Turner, along with a copy of the Farmers Weekly report on the event. Needless to say, our new sales and marketing director was somewhat displeased and, as was his way, he made his displeasure known in no uncertain manner.

I hastily arranged a meeting with Levertons' sales manager, Bill Osgothorpe, at which it was quite clear that they had gone into the event not realising its significance. They had used a brand new tractor that was inadequately prepared for ordinary

TOP:
Dealer Lammings of Surfleet received good support from the Leyland sales and demonstration team of, left to right, Alan Hawes, me, Ray Runciman, Jim Lawson, Peter Blair and Brian Webb.
© *British Motor Industry Heritage Trust*

CENTRE:
Along with Alan Hawes, centre, I am keeping a close eye on the work of the Long Sutton Tractor Trials' scrutineer, left, as he counts the tractor's wheel revolutions.
© *British Motor Industry Heritage Trust*

LEFT:
Ploughing at the Long Sutton Tractor Trials in 1978, a two-wheel drive Leyland 272 Synchro achieved a remarkably low wheel-slip figure of just 5.7%.
© *British Motor Industry Heritage Trust*

field work, let alone a highly competitive public demonstration. It also had a plough with which they were totally unfamiliar and basically it was a recipe for disaster in demonstration terms.

Out of this meeting came an agreement that if the event was to be staged again the following year, which it was, then Levertons would complete the entry form and Leyland would do everything else.

Not only was there a Long Sutton Tractor Trials held in 1971, but it continued up to the mid-1980s. To those who never had the good fortune to visit the trials, they were always incredibly well organised and attended by several thousand farmers from over a wide area. From a manufacturer's viewpoint they always attracted heaps of valuable publicity.

In 1971 it fell to Brian Webb and myself to organise Leyland's participation at the event. This time, though, we had one of our own factory demonstrator 384s to call on. We equipped it with 14 x 30 rears on PAVT wheels, water ballasted all round, and plenty of front-end weights.

Our only concession to Levertons was an agreement to use the same plough as the previous year – a Barford. This was one of a small range offered at the time by Barford of Belton, a sister company in the British Leyland group. Although Brian disliked the quality of the work it produced (he was a Ransomes man through and through) we had identified that it was lower in draught than many ploughs of its size.

To cut a very long story short, it is always attention to detail that made the difference at these demonstrations. On this occasion the 384 was credited with 7% wheel slip, the lowest on the day. Perhaps modesty ought to prevent me from saying much more on this subject, but what the heck!

A stock 72hp Leyland 272 from dealers Lammings of Surfleet on static display at the Long Sutton Tractor Trials, probably in 1978. © *British Motor Industry Heritage Trust*

Our wheel-slip was less than a pair of Muir-Hills and a Roadless 115, which recorded 8%, 10% and 12% respectively. The Ford 5000 came away with 19%, the MF 185 with 23%, and the IH 574 with 35%.

I don't recall receiving a memo from Bob Turner that year, but then neither Brian nor I wanted one. We had done what we set out to do and the resulting good publicity for Leyland was all that mattered. Through the 1970s the Leyland team achieved wheel-slip figures as low as 5.7% (1978 with a 272), better than many four-wheel drive tractors, which by this time were making increasingly considerable inroads into the UK market.

By this time, the Long Sutton organisers had introduced optional tests for PTO hp and in-cab noise levels, though some manufacturers declined to enter these.

By this time I was based at the Tractor Training School at Mosside Farm, Bathgate, where I was responsible for writing the regular newsletters to the distributors. I remember commenting that several competitors including Zetor, Fendt and Lamborghini had declined the decibel test. I suggested that Leyland salesmen up and down the country should draw their own conclusions from this. I finished by asking: 'And what about Deutz?' They were neither seen, nor heard, anywhere!

Earlier in my story I mentioned how, under Bob Turner's leadership, British Leyland's Tractor Division moved its sales and marketing departments from Longbridge to Bathgate in late 1968. And what an eminently sensible move that turned out to be.

Following the closure of the original Nuffield factory at Ward End, Birmingham, our service division had been grouped with all the other BMC/British Leyland service departments at Cowley. As part of the centralisation process, the service division also made the move north to new offices within the Bathgate factory complex.

For the very first time, the departments with responsibilities for tractor sales, marketing and service were based on the same site. The exception to this centralisation was the all-important parts division, which continued to be based within the huge, fully-automated parts warehouse at Cowley.

The advantages of centralising all these departments at Bathgate soon became apparent. Not only did it create a much closer working relationship between the team whose job it was to promote and increase sales of the Leyland tractor range, it also ensured the highest possible levels of customer service and satisfaction.

A few new names and faces began to appear in the service department including service manager David Ebrey and Alan Hawes, who was appointed as an office-based technical advisor. Andy McMeechan moved away from a position within the factory to become a field service engineer covering Scotland, northern England and Northern Ireland. Over the years he became highly respected by dealers and farmers alike.

A new tractor training school was established on the western edge of the Bathgate factory. The land on which the factory had been built six or seven years earlier was known as Mosside Farm and some of the farm buildings still survived. These were refurbished, modernised and converted into workshops, lecture rooms and offices.

Initially, the school was managed by John Arkell, who some years earlier had left Leyland to work for New Holland, before returning to the company, and he was followed by Ron Kettle.

The tractor training school welcomed many hundreds of people from all over the world through its doors. In the late 1970s I moved to Scotland with my wife and two sons, where I took over as product training manager at the school when Ron moved into export sales. Neil Spalding and John Paterson were two of the lecturers, and it can truly be said that what they didn't know about Leyland tractors wasn't worth knowing! Typically, they would strip a tractor down to its very last nut and bolt and rebuild it in times far shorter than those laid down in official repair time schedules.

During my time in Bathgate, the training school continued to operate on a truly world-wide basis, with sales and service personnel attending from Australia, New Zealand, Malaysia, the USA and Canada, all four Scandinavian countries, Morocco, Turkey, Greece, Italy, France, Holland and Eire to name but a few. All those who attended were great people to work and to socialise with – they knew the product well and were determined to see it succeed in their own home market. The same, of course, could also be said of those who came to us from dealerships in the UK.

Mosside Farm was also established as the base for the tractor demonstration unit, operating at the time with a fleet of up to 15 or 20 tractors. Bobby Twaddle was in charge of the day-to-day running of this unit. His team of demonstrators included such personalities as Ray Runciman, George Livingstone, Ian Jack and Jim Lawson. Jim drove our 40ft articulated lorry with its specially designed trailer capable of carrying three of the largest tractors in the range. While the tractors rarely left these shores, apart from regular trips to Northern Ireland, Bobby went to Morocco on two occasions, and Ray, George and Ian made various trips into Europe and Scandinavia to help promote sales in those all-important export markets.

Talking of Morocco reminds me of the time that Ron Kettle and I were nominated to go out there by our boss, Bob Turner. It transpired that Bob and his export sales staff had successfully concluded a massive order for 500 Leyland 272s (two-wheel drive, 72hp). Nuffield and Leyland tractors weren't completely unknown in Morocco, but this order was a considerable increase over what had gone there before.

Oddly enough the importer, Berliet Maroc, was a subsidiary of Renault in France which, looking back, made the order all the more of an achievement. Be that as it may, a condition of the order called for sales and training support to be supplied, which is where Ron and I came in. We spent almost three weeks in and around Rabat, just to the south of Casablanca, providing theoretical and practical product training for groups of salesmen and service engineers from the various dealers around the country, contracted by Berliet Maroc to retail the tractors.

These dealers had previously been selling a variety of different tractor marques, all cabless and even without safety frames. It quickly became obvious to Ron and me that the dealers who had been accustomed to selling Fords and Masseys were more difficult to deal with in terms of convincing them of the superior features and benefits provided by the Leyland 272.

French was, and still is, the everyday language in Morocco. One man, from an MF dealership, steadfastly refused to accept our sales patter, even to the extent of talking to us in Arabic, which we certainly did not understand. We could conduct a reasonable conversation in French, but we barely knew a word of Arabic. In spite of the semi-tropical temperatures, this man always wore a knitted hat, which duly earned him the nickname Woolly Hat.

We had numerous verbal tussles with him over specification comparisons, and it was only when we went into the field with a variety of locally produced implements that he began to grudgingly admit that his beloved MF 165 did not perform quite as well as the Leyland 272. Such characters are to be found in all parts of the world; they were generally to be admired and certainly added to the challenge and enjoyment of the job.

The 272s we supplied to Morocco were fitted with the Bathgate-built Leyland 98 Series engine. When its predecessor, the 38TD range, reached the end of its long production life, it began to become slightly troublesome in operation. After all, it was pushing out far more horses than it was originally designed for.

The 38TD designation indicated a capacity of 3.8 litres, which was achieved with a bore of 100mm and a stroke of 120mm; it was by the standards of the day a long-stroke, high-torque power unit. Its replacement, the 98 Series, retained the same swept volume, but the bore was reduced to 98mm, hence the designation, and the stroke increased to 125mm. The new engine's bore-to-stroke ratio was, therefore,

TOP:
Leyland's impressive demonstration unit prepares to leave Bathgate in the late 1970s with a cargo of Synchro tractors, left to right, 245, 262 and 462.
© *British Motor Industry Heritage Trust*

BELOW LEFT:
'Tractors for all seasons' was the message Bob Twaddle, left, and Martin Stokes took with them to Northern Ireland in 1979. A ferry journey was a rare event for the demonstration unit, which rarely ventured outside the British Isles.
© *British Motor Industry Heritage Trust*

BELOW RIGHT:
During the late 1970s Leyland's tractor demonstration unit was manned by, left to right, Jim Lawson, team leader Bob Twaddle and Ian Jack.
© *British Motor Industry Heritage Trust*

even better. It provided higher maximum torque figures at lower revolutions, together with more frugal fuel consumption than its predecessor. The engine's torque and fuel consumption figures were better than many of our competitors, some of whom, notably Ford, John Deere and Fiat, appeared to have followed truck philosophy and moved over to high-revving, over-square power unit.

I don't know much about the engine configurations used by manufacturers today, but in the 1970s and 1980s those of us working for Leyland had absolutely no doubt that the 98 Series engines were, horsepower for horsepower, superior to anything else in the marketplace. The six-cylinder versions of the 98 Series, and their applications in the Leyland range, were another matter.

Revisiting some of the sales we achieved, it's clear that the early years following the change from Nuffield to Leyland were some of the most productive and successful

TOP:
As part of a deal to support an order for 500 tractors, I spent three weeks in Morocco with Ron Kettle in 1977 providing technical support and advice to dealers on the operational benefits of the Leyland 272.
© *Name Surname*

RIGHT:
Six-cylinder tractors launched by Leyland in 1973 included the 2100 (two-wheel drive/100hp). This photograph was taken in the Penecuik Studio, near Edinburgh, where Ron Kettle and I spent several weeks preparing new sales brochures.
© *British Motor Industry Heritage Trust*

in the history of this famous British marque. One or two figures, particularly for export sales, make interesting reading when related to present-day market conditions and the levels, or absence of them, of UK tractor production.

For instance, in 1971 some 2000 tractors were exported to the USA and over 500 to Venezuela. In 1973 Mexico was opened up as a new market and an initial 100 units were dispatched towards the end of that year, and another 500 went to India. We also shipped 1200 tractors out to Australia during 1975. These are figures that I've picked out at random from a long list of on-going export business that included virtually all European and certainly all Scandinavian markets. Large orders were obtained from South America, Canada and New Zealand, as well as several countries in Asia and the Middle East, including Egypt, Sudan and Tunisia.

By 1978 Columbia had accounted for over 1000 units, Venezuela 1500 and South Africa 3500. In 1979 we sold 222 tractors in Italy, one of the most prolific foreign nations when it came to producing tractors. I have it from a very reliable source that there are, even today, over 5000 Nuffield and Leyland tractors still at work on farms in this country. How times – and the balances of trade – have changed.

In our own home market, Leyland became a more acceptable name than Nuffield, and sales were made to customers who in the past had, for reasons I find difficult to define, never been prepared to consider an orange tractor. By the early 1970s the 70hp sector, while still forming a large part of sales in the UK, was beginning to be matched and gradually overtaken by more powerful units, typified by the four-cylinder turbo Ford 7000.

At that time turbo-charging was relatively new to the world of agricultural tractors and there was a degree of resistance to it. It was seen by some, and promoted by Ford's competitors, as being an attempt to get a quart out of the proverbial pint pot.

In relaxed mood at the Edinburgh photographic studio, left to right, studio owner; Peter Fogg, tractor marketing manager; John Wigham, marketing assistant; Ron Kettle; Ernie (photographer); Dave Turner export sales (behind tractor); me.
© *British Motor Industry Heritage Trust*

Today, of course, the technology has improved and with it the wholesale acceptability of the principle.

At Leyland, within the secretive corridors of Bathgate's department of product planning, this trend towards higher horsepower had not only been noted, but was being acted upon. No doubt the course taken by Ford (turbo-charging) would have been considered, evaluated and, possibly, it would have been quickly rejected. As I have already mentioned on one or two occasions, the Bathgate factory produced not only tractors but a range of both four- and, importantly, six-cylinder engines as well.

Why try to get the quart that farmers were now wanting out of a four-cylinder pot, when from the same Bathgate production line it was possible to get a very much larger pot with six cylinders? This probably isn't the way it happened in reality, but it was generally agreed that a proven, big-capacity six-cylinder engine would be a far more attractive proposition in market places around the world than a turbo-charged four-cylinder.

The engine in question was, of course, the long-stroke, low-revving, high-torque Leyland 6/98 with a capacity of 5.8 litres. It had all the right characteristics needed for tractors in the top end of the horsepower bracket. And, it was argued, it needn't be any more expensive.

We decided to launch the new tractors at the 1973 Royal Smithfield Show. While the engineers and production people were doing their bit leading up to the official launch, a small team, including Ron Kettle, myself and Ernie, our top in-house photographer from the Nuffield Press at Cowley, spent several weeks in a photographic studio at Penecuick, just outside Edinburgh, doing the necessary work for the new brochures.

At least one Leyland 2100 was converted into unequal-wheel four-wheel drive by our French importer. It used a Carraro axle and was called the 2100-4. © *British Motor Industry Heritage Trust*

These brochures were being designed by an agency in Edinburgh, and Ron and I were asked to check over the accompanying story lines. To put it mildly, we were not impressed and we said so. Apart from incurring the considerable wrath of the agency man who had done the original text work, Ron and I were tasked with rewriting the script. A great deal of midnight oil was burnt to meet the tight deadlines.

TOP:
The Leyland 262H and 272H models featured a very reliable 11-tooth pinion that Brian Webb and I specifically requested as an option to the troublesome nine-tooth pinion that was giving problems in our arable areas.
© *British Motor Industry Heritage Trust*

LEFT:
The 'H' suffix on the Leyland 262H, pictured, and 272H models Leyland denoted that they were fitted with a high ratio 11-tooth pinion.
© *British Motor Industry Heritage Trust*

In virtually every market, both at home and abroad, the concept was greeted with enthusiasm. The Leyland 285 and 2100 were among the first British-made tractors to be powered by six-cylinder engines; they also had spacious cabs with an almost flat floor, side-mounted gear levers and, new to Leyland, oil-immersed brakes and epicyclic final drives. These last two components were bought-in items from County Commercial Cars of Fleet in Hampshire.

The launch took place at the 1973 Royal Smithfield Show, where I well remember the stand being chaotic from the beginning to the end of the week. It was mobbed by huge numbers of farmers, drivers and gentlemen of the press. The two new models, together with their four-wheel drive counterparts, the 485 and 4100, were unveiled under the banner 'Leyland – The New Power in Tractors'.

With the considerable benefit of hindsight, it can truthfully be said that the engine was the easy bit! When introducing a new range of high-hp tractors, the product planning department would have recognised that a balanced package of other major components was needed – clutch, transmission, braking, PTO, hydraulics and cab, for example. To say that this balance, particularly in respect of the transmission, was not achieved would be an understatement.

The ten-speed gearbox, as used very successfully in the three- and four-cylinder tractors, was up-rated in several aspects of its specification. It was, however, an ageing design. Improvements such as there were, which I could, at best, only describe as cosmetic, could not

TOP:
The Ton Webb, a dealer-fitted assistor ram kit for the Leyland 262/272, was a joint effort between myself and Brian Webb. It was manufactured and supplied by Leyland dealer R. Chambers of Scarcliffe, Chesterfield.

RIGHT:
Had the Leyland 285 and 2100 models not experienced recurring mechanical difficulties, they might have been a winner on shaft work. Their failure left the 282 (82hp) to carry the firm's high-hp fight.

in any way provide the transmission with the characteristics required to match the power and torque output from the 6/98 engines.

Almost from day one, Leyland 285 and 2100 (two-wheel drive, 85hp and 100hp respectively) tractors that were used for ploughing and cultivation began to suffer from gearbox problems. Forty years on it is difficult, if not impossible, to know in which direction to point any accusing finger. And after such a long period of time perhaps it doesn't really matter.

Had sufficient prototype testing work been carried out and, if so, had it been with suitable implements in really tough going? Perhaps the pressure from above to get the new models into production was just too great? There may even have been a lack of understanding in some quarters as to what tractors of this size and power were expected to do. Whatever the cause or reason, the concept itself – to produce a range of tractors in the 85-100hp sector – was spot on. The execution, however, was definitely wide of the mark.

As the 1970s progressed my time as a territory-based area manager was approaching its end, with an office desk being talked about as the next step in my promotion ladder. This, of course, had certain attractions, perhaps not the least of which were financial.

But before I touch on my involvement with the Leyland tractor range from inside an office, rather than from outside, there are still one or two episodes which I and some of my colleagues found interesting at the time, and which I think are worthy of relating.

I don't know whether it applied to other tractor manufacturers, but working on territory for Leyland did permit a degree of flexibility in your daily routine. This flexibility allowed individuals to devote time to aspects of the business which, in the strictest sense, were not included in the job description. This we always did with the best interests of the success of the product as the sole aim. Two such instances in which Brian Webb and I worked together come to mind.

Earlier in my story, while describing the introduction of the ten-speed transmission which brought about the launch of the Nuffield 10/60 and 10/42, I made mention of the change to the final drive design which was felt necessary at that time. I also mentioned how this new final drive was less capable of withstanding the stresses of heavy arable farming than the original arrangement designed for the Nuffield five-speed box it replaced.

In parts of the country where heavy land predominated, Nuffield and Leyland lost sales as a result of this weakness, which was a failure of the nine-tooth final drive pinion. Earlier five-speed tractors had always been fitted with an 11-tooth pinion, which had given trouble-free service over many years.

It so happened that the 11-tooth pinion, as a component, had been retained in production and was being fitted to the skid units supplied to JCB, Hymac, Coventry Climax and other industrial users. A diff-lock wasn't specified for these applications, and the pinion was produced without the splines that would otherwise enable the differential to be locked.

The crux of this story revolves around the fact that I was responsible for sales through distributors who, in the main, sold to customers with heavy land arable farms.

And it was these same distributors who were seeing their sales decline as a result. They included Robert B. Massey at Market Weighton, Lyons of Gainsborough, F. C. Jackson at Coningsby, Fenton & Townsend at Sleaford, the F. H. Burgess branches at Horncastle and Louth and, outside my area of responsibility, in Essex, through Blyth & Pawsey.

For some ten years following the introduction of the Nuffield 10/60 the sale of our 60hp to 70hp tractors for heavy arable work declined as a result of the pinion problem, and with it the level of tractor business being done by our distributors. This happened to such an extent that the powers-that-be at Bathgate would argue that the problem did not exist, and on paper it didn't! I argued that the only reason it didn't exist anymore was because we were no longer selling tractors in those areas for applications that gave rise to the problem.

Leyland's home sales manager in the early 1970s was Jim Taylor, and it was he alone who showed any real concern and understanding of the problem. I suggested to him that we should fit our 70hp tractor with the 11-tooth pinions, not to test them for their reliability, because I had no fears from that standpoint, but to check what effect they would have on the workability of the tractor as far as the changes to the gear ratios were concerned. Jim agreed to this, and we duly dispatched a 270 demonstration tractor to Newark in Nottinghamshire.

Together with my colleague, Brian Webb, I obtained the necessary bull gears and pinions during a convenient visit to Bathgate, and a few days later supervised their fitting in the workshops of J. L. Maltby, the Leyland distributor at Newark.

The tractor was then put to work on local farms doing a variety of jobs and over the weeks the feedback was almost entirely positive. To cut a long story short, Jim Taylor was suitably impressed with the contents of the reports we submitted. He persuaded both the engineering and production departments in Bathgate that the 11-tooth pinion final drive arrangement, complete with differential lock, of course, should be made available as an option to the standard arrangement. So it was that special versions of both the 62hp and 72hp tractors, known respectively as the 262H and 272H, were introduced.

Surprising as it may seem in this day and age, 40 years ago a three-furrow reversible plough was, by and large, the norm on the majority of arable farms. For many years the bench-mark manufacturer of both conventional and reversible ploughs was Ipswich-based Ransomes.

For several years the TS83 three-furrow reversible plough was a market leader for Ransomes. We demonstrated our tractors with this plough on frequent occasions; it was featured in Nuffield literature and it matched the hydraulic capabilities of both Nuffield and Leyland tractors extremely well, this being in spite of the close marketing arrangements between Ransomes and Ford at that time.

Then one day Ransomes announced a successor to the TS83 – the TS103. It was an all-new three-furrow reversible unit, more robustly built than its predecessor, with a frame manufactured from square box section, longer and, importantly, heavier.

On the face of it, the TS103 was still within the capabilities of the Leyland's hydralic lift system, but you know how it is! You might be autumn ploughing after a crop of sugar beet has been lifted, perhaps the land is just on the side of being too wet for the job, but the Leyland 270 or perhaps the new 272 keeps pulling through, as it always does.

You keep going into the early evening and everything about the tractor, including the hydraulic/transmission oil, is nicely warmed up, and you begin to notice that your new TS103 plough is not lifting quite as quickly as it did first thing in the morning.

Well, with time we came to learn that the TS103 was too close to the operational limit of our hydraulic system for complete comfort. Once again those of us with the responsibility for sales found ourselves hitting a brick wall at Bathgate when we mentioned increased lift capacity, or suggested the need for an assistor ram. On this occasion we had not only Jim Taylor but also Bob Turner (both ex-Ford men) on our side, with both saying very definitely that the Ransomes TS103 was the market leader in its class, and how it was essential that our hydraulic system should be completely compatible. But still the months went by with no sign of improvement.

So Brian Webb and I put our heads together again. Brian, with the benefit of having completed an engineering course at Lackham College, came up with not only a design for an assistor ram, but also a wooden mock-up as well. Again, with the knowledge and blessing of Jim Taylor, we set to work; this time it was at R. Chambers, a small, but very well-equipped distributor at Scarcliffe, near Chesterfield.

What Dick Chambers and his staff didn't know about top-class welding, profile cutting and metal fabrication wasn't worth knowing. Before long, Brian's wooden mock-up was transformed into a heavy duty metal bracket (when Bathgate design staff saw it they described it as being 'over-engineered') which mounted on the half-axle casing and formed the anchor point of a ram of the type used on the Leyland 285 and 2100 tractors.

Open-air driving had a certain charm and I still have fond memories of the time I spent driving tractors like the Field Marshall Series I.

85

Subsequent field-testing, mainly on David Cheetham's farm at Bevercotes in Nottinghamshire, proved the correctness of the original design, and it has to be said that over the years Dick Chambers supplied several hundred of what, unofficially, became known as the TonWebb Assistor Ram Kit.

More importantly, the Ransomes TS103 and similar new ploughs from other manufacturers were brought safely within the hydraulic limits of Leyland's 70hp tractors. Interestingly, it wasn't until the introduction of the Leyland 282 and 482 in 1979 that a factory-fitted assistor ram of in-house design became available.

TOP:
The 47hp Leyland 253 had a tilt-back safety cab that was initially made by Sta-Dri, then from late 1972 by Victor Cabs of Broseley, Shropshire.
© British Motor Industry Heritage Trust

RIGHT:
Leyland sub-contracted its cab manufacturing work out to West Midlands firm Victor Cabs (latterly Air Flow Streamline). Victor Cabs employed 196 people producing 40 cabs a day for a variety of manufacturers.

I have often mentioned the time when, as a nation, we exported more tractors than all the other countries in the world put together. Naturally, I've usually made some mention of the contribution made by both Nuffield and Leyland to the happy and prosperous strength of the British economy during the 1960s and 70s. From where does our economic strength and prosperity come now if, as a nation, we continue to import more capital goods than we export?

So far, though, I've failed to mention the Republic of Ireland and Northern Ireland – export destinations with which Nuffield, Leyland and, latterly, Marshall enjoyed a long and successful association. Therefore I thought I would write a few lines about the people who supported our products across the Irish Sea.

For those of us who handled the sales and service responsibilities for these territories, enjoyment would be the right word to use to describe our fruitful association with the Irish. Nuffield and Leyland tractors have always been, and doubtless still are, very popular on both sides of the border in that green and pleasant island.

I became involved with the Irish market during my time as product training manager at Leyland's Bathgate plant. Our Leyland importer in the Republic was Mahon & McPhillips in Kilkenny. In their heyday they would import up to 400 Bathgate-built tractors a year which, taking into account the total size of that relatively small country, was quite a considerable quantity.

Their managing director was Ned Mahon and sales were the responsibility of Dick Hanrahan. As was so often the case with the importers of our tractors, not just locally but all over the world, both Ned and Dick had complete faith in the superiority of the Birmingham-built Nuffield range and the later Bathgate-built tractors.

With the professional support of a capable and efficiently-run service department, headed up by Paddy Heeley and Liam Murphy, and a parts division managed by Mat Dooley, Mahon & McPhillips sold a vast number of Nuffield and Leyland tractors. Their influence extended out through a network of dealers stretching from Cork to Donegal and from Wexford and Wicklow across to the Atlantic coast.

One of these dealers was Alfie Spencer of Springmount Tractors, Gorey in Co. Wexford. A few years ago he reminded me how, in 1979, he once sold no fewer than five Leyland 272 Synchro tractors in one week! As a matter of interest, at least two of those five tractors are still at work today on the same farms they went to 33 years ago.

Alfie Spencer continued his association with the product right up to and including the Steyr-based Marshalls of the late 1980s and very early 90s. He was still retailing Steyr tractors up until a few years ago.

Also notable among the Irish dealers were Jack Whelan from Co. Clare, Michael Hudson from Co. Wicklow and Joe Ahern from the Limerick area. I haven't spoken to Joe for many years, although I'm told he still believes Nuffield and Leyland tractors were the finest machines on the planet.

In terms of our own support team for the area, Scotsman Val Muir was appointed as regional manager with responsibility for overseeing sales in both the Republic and Northern Ireland.

He did this very effectively – in his own inimitable style, of course – for a period of several years. A similarly strong relationship was developed on the technical service side where David Ebrey, our Bathgate-based service manager, was always on hand to smooth over and resolve the inevitable technical problems that arose. North of the border he was backed up by either Martin Stokes or Andy McMeechan.

Nuffield and Leyland tractors were thought of just as highly north of the border. The original Nuffield distributor was Stephenson Bros of Lisburn, who also ran a small branch in Cookstown. Stephenson Bros were also New Holland dealers in the days when NH were known largely for the quality of their balers, mowers etc. They stocked and sold a small range of ancillary equipment for tractors, notably the Horndraulic range of front-end loaders.

Stephenson Bros also held some of the BMC and British Leyland car franchises, including Morris and Wolseley. This wasn't an ideal scenario as, in terms of the level of effort put aside for their promotion, tractors often came off second best to cars. Neither Jack Stephenson nor his sales director, Hugh Collins, would admit this was true, but their falling tractor sales began to confirm it was, indeed, the case.

At some time during Val Muir's reign, Stephenson Bros were persuaded that they weren't going to be able to cope with the increasing levels of competition in the Northern Ireland tractor market. The outcome of the discussions Val had with Jack and Hugh was the appointment of Kane & McPherson at Ballycastle. This appointment ensured that Leyland now had the backing of a much more aggressive and dedicated dealership. As a result, our sales began to show a steep upward curve, an ascendance that continued right through until the end of the Marshall era in the mid-1980s.

Making a valuable contribution to this increase in sales in Northern Ireland was a network of dealers, some new to the range, others who had been involved with the marque since the early days of Nuffield. Typical of the latter was T. A. (Tommy) Simms in Co. Armagh, and Linton & Robinson at Strabane. They were joined by relative newcomers, Ivan Allen at Banbridge and Timothy McFarland at Fintona.

As was the case with Alfie Spencer, Timothy McFarland's association with Leyland and latterly Marshall continued right through to the Steyr-based range. We, this is Andy McMeechan and myself, introduced him to the range in the late 1980s and he continued to import tractors from Austria when the Marshall/Steyr agreement came to an end in the early 1990s.

Hindsight, as the saying goes, is a wonderful thing. As strong as sales were within Ireland, I can only wonder what would have happened to Leyland's sales figures had the six-cylinder 285 and 2100 models of the mid-1970s been the success story they should have been?

In my opinion, Irish farmers always led the way in terms of their unquenchable thirst for more horsepower, particularly at the PTO shaft. Timothy McFarland's sales of self-propelled forage harvesters were and probably still are an indication of the need for high-horsepower, high-output machines for grass harvesting. Leyland's 285 and 2100 tractors – compact, economical and with plenty of power and torque – should have been ideal tractors for the Irish market. What a tragedy they failed to live up to everyone's expectations.

As a result of the Leyland 285 and 2100's poor record of reliability, and their subsequent failure to achieve a decent level of market penetration, it left the firm's established four-cylinder tractors in a position where they had to fight it out with the competition.

The relationship between the Emerald Isle and Nuffield, Leyland and Marshall tractors was, in the main, long and fruitful. On a personal note I still feel honoured to have been able to play a part in the formulation of this special relationship. It is without doubt a period of time that has contributed considerably to the many pleasant recollections that I have from my career spent working for Nuffield, Leyland and Marshall.

TOP:
This cab transporter was a familiar sight on the motorways as it travelled between Air Flow Streamline's West Midlands factory and the Leyland tractor plant in Bathgate, Scotland.

LEFT:
Leyland's 245 (47hp) tractor fitted with the company's Q cab. Mounted on rubber bushes, the cab had a rating of 85dBA.
© *British Motor Industry Heritage Trust*

Having reached my mid-70s, I can count myself fortunate enough to be able to remember those halcyon days before our lords and masters in Whitehall and Brussels ruled that all new tractors should be fitted with a protective cab. Of course, I was always in favour of the protection provided by the first safety cabs, even though they were sounding boxes that amplified engine and transmission noise to the detriment of the hearing of many thousands of tractor drivers.

I can remember with some fondness the joys of driving Fordson Standards, Fordson Majors, single-cylinder Marshalls, Ferguson TE-20s and, of course, various Nuffield and Leyland models. That was in the days when drivers were considered to be made of sterner stuff than appears to be the case nowadays!

What used to be termed weather cabs were available from such manufacturers as Winsam, Duncan, Sta-Dri, Lambourn, Tractor-Vision and others. Early Duncan cabs were clad with plywood and the Lambourn almost entirely with a heavy green canvas. All these cabs had to be fitted either by the supplying dealer or the farmer himself.

Exactly what proportion of new tractors were sold complete with a weather cab was probably never recorded; in my experience unless the tractor was to be driven mainly by the farmer himself, or perhaps by one of his sons, then that particular tractor remained cableless.

Be that as it may, come rain, snow or shine there was always a feeling of elation from being exposed to the elements. Just think of it – no heater, no air-conditioning, no wireless (or is it called radio, these days?), no air-sprung seat with adjustable suspension and, of course, no windscreen.

An old Leyland colleague of mine used to say that he had a sack of hay for his tractor seat cushion and this same sack went on his head when it rained. In my experience a good, long oil-skin coat, warm weatherproof gloves and wellies were almost all you wanted in winter; in summer you could wear as little as you liked – well, almost.

Was it healthier into the bargain? I think so. In the seven years I spent working on farms in the 1950s and early 60s I don't think I ever had an attack of the 'flu or a serious cold. However, during my first few weeks in the Nuffield sales office at Cowley, in January 1962, I had one cold after another. Admittedly, there were some heavy smokers about and passive smoking hadn't even been invented by then.

The very sensible introduction of the safety cab as a legal requirement was followed quite quickly by the equally sensible requirement to bring noise levels down to a maximum of 90 decibels at the driver's ear. Leyland Tractors introduced their first Q cab in 1976, the same year that the automatic hitch became a standard fitting.

Whereas previously all cabs were designed as simple bolt-on additions to the basic tractor, the quiet cab had to be designed from the ground up as a completely separate entity. To my mind it represented the first major departure from what had always been, irrespective of make, a fairly simple piece of engineering: two smaller wheels at the front, two larger ones at the back and the engine, gear-box and hydraulics, together with the driver, slung in between.

The engagement or actuation of the clutch, brakes, steering, diff-lock, power take-off and hydraulics had always been simple and uncomplicated. Now, however, in order to comply with what were then quite stringent noise standards, everything had to be changed; hydraulic actuation of most controls became the order of the day. For the first time hydrostatic as opposed to power-assisted steering became standard almost across the board.

Those of us with the responsibility for promoting the Leyland range were, with some justification, proud of what our designers and engineers in Bathgate had come up with in order to meet the new legislation. The Leyland Q cab design had gone through a lengthy development period: a new cab trim area had to be set up within B block and the production line itself had to be lengthened by some 20 yards to enable on-line fitment.

In parallel with this activity at Bathgate, examples of the cab had to be submitted to the cab test centre at the NIAE at Silsoe, where they underwent crush, impact and noise-level testing. I well remember one of the officials there confiding in me that if he ever had to choose which tractor he would prefer to have a roll-over accident in, it would without any shadow of a doubt be a Leyland.

The basic frame of the cab, being little more than a very substantial metal fabrication, wasn't produced in Bathgate. Instead, the manufacturing work was sub-contracted out to a company in the West Midlands called Victor Cabs (latterly Air Flow Stream-line), which fabricated the basic shell and painted and glazed it in their own works. Batches of 20 cabs were then loaded on to specially designed articulated trailers and despatched to their next port of call, the Bathgate factory and its newly established cab trim area.

Once at Bathgate, assembly workers in B block added the components that were necessary to operate the tractor. These included the all-important clutch, brake and diff-lock pedals, as well as the hydraulic quadrant, hydrostatic steering, cab heater (an innovation!), and an adjustable sprung seat. Thick floor matting and other items of noise-absorbent trim were also added at this time.

The result was a quality, well-finished cab that was much liked by farmers and drivers and not just in the UK. Scandinavia, for example, had some of the strictest noise laws in Europe, yet it was one of Leyland's largest export markets.

The introduction of the Q cab to home market dealers was held on a farm just outside Stratford-on-Avon, and it was left very much to Brian Webb and myself to organise the launch. A variety of implements was assembled to enable us to load the tractors to their maximum limit. To further emphasise the advantages of having a quiet cab, Martin Stokes and Andy McMeechan were on hand to demonstrate how easily the new cabs could be removed if clutch or transmission repairs were needed. They carried out the demonstration in the middle of one of the fields, with the help of a mobile gantry. The cab was duly removed from a working tractor and replaced within an hour.

One little recollection from the day is worthy of note. Brian Webb, our chief demonstrator, lived very close to the site and for whatever reason he chose to bring along his three-year-old daughter, Jackie, to one of the demonstrations. Although it wasn't strictly legal to have her there in the cab, she nevertheless fell asleep while Brian ploughed out the field boundaries. What better proof of the sound insulating abilities and comfort offered by the Leyland quiet cab?

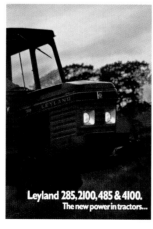

Leyland's sales literature of the 1970s was always well designed and printed on good quality glossy paper. The Q cab brochure, *far right*, was distributed as an insert in a number of farming magazines during mid-1976.
© *British Motor Industry Heritage Trust*

Seven
Shifting
up a Gear

By the mid-1970s the standard specifications of most makes and models of UK-built tractors were becoming ever more comprehensive. Items that had always been available as optional extras were sometimes ordered, but more often than not they were ignored because of the additional retail cost.

How many of us, for instance, can remember driving a tractor without some form of power steering, even when a front-end loader was fitted?

Pick-up hitches were few and far between, even in the late 60s and early 70s, and as far as Leyland was concerned they didn't become a factory-fitted component until 1976. Prior to this, the swinging drawbar was the norm, while a somewhat rudimentary auto-hitch made by ARM (Agricultural Requisites and Mechanisation) was only available as a dealer-fitted accessory.

Around this time, even relatively low-cost components had to be ordered as factory-fitted extras. Tipping trailer pipes with Dowty or Exactor screw-on type couplings were one example of useful extras that perhaps should have been standard equipment. Double-acting valves and quick-release couplings were another and were virtually unknown from any manufacturer.

The first quiet cabs, in most cases, were fitted with a heater, but little thought was given to the need for in-cab entertainment and no thought at all to air-conditioning. However, during the second half of the 1970s most manufacturers adopted policies of building many of these previously optional items into the standard spec of their tractor models.

Looking back now, it's amazing how times and specifications have changed during the intervening years.

All the above items, apart from the Q cab itself, were optional and had to be specified and paid for if required. But what about the structure of the tractor – the backbone of the engine, clutch, transmission and hydraulics? What, if anything, was happening to this?

In the case of most manufacturers the answer would be 'not very much'.

Several evolutionary increases in horsepower had occurred at Leyland, and some important changes to the design of the four-cylinder engine had culminated in the highly successful and popular 4/98 Series. In parallel with this, several other changes were being introduced into the Leyland hydraulic system, including dual-flow hydraulic pumps and single-lever control for both draught and position. However, it must be said they were hardly of world-shattering importance.

Let it not be thought, however, that bright ideas were scarce within Bathgate's product planning, design and engineering departments, or that there was a shortage of revolutionary thinking.

It may be, however, that the powers that be who controlled the purse-strings of new product investment sometimes paid too much attention to a maxim often quoted by the principal of the Nottinghamshire Agricultural College, which I attended in the early 50s. The principal, Philip Lythe, frequently warned us would-be farmers and farmers' sons 'not to be the first to try the new, nor yet the last to use the old'.

In view of the fact that the first synchromesh transmissions for tractors were introduced in around 1973 by the likes of International Harvester, David Brown, Fiat, Deutz and Same, Leyland certainly couldn't claim to be the first out of the blocks with a synchromesh transmission. But then again, we were far from being the last.

TOP:
Leyland's pre-synchromesh tractor range relied on gearbox technology that descended from the original Nuffield Universal of 1948. This 272 dates from 1976-1978.
© *British Motor Industry Heritage Trust*

RIGHT:
Leyland's Synchro tractor range, comprising the 245, 262 and 272 models, featured the same styling as their predecessors.
© *British Motor Industry Heritage Trust*

Leyland's Synchro transmission was launched to the world during February and March of 1978 and at that time neither Ford, MF nor John Deere offered synchro-mesh anywhere in their ranges. The Synchro transmission replaced the previous Nuffield-designed 10-speed gearbox which, in turn, owed its parentage to the original five-speed transmission designed for the first Nuffield Universal of 1948, a highly successful life-span of 30 years.

But if the Synchro transmission became public in 1978, its conception on the brightly-lit, widely-spaced drawing boards at Bathgate began to take place at least four years earlier. The senior transmission engineer was a young Welshman called Simon Evans. With a small team, he was given the task of designing a new transmission that would take Leyland tractors into the 1980s and beyond, or so it seemed at the time.

Bob Beresford, then product engineering director, together with Ralph Wiggington and Mike Barnes, were all involved in the programme. Simon, however, had the main responsibility and, as sometimes happens when individuals are required to concentrate on one major project and live with it right through to fruition, nicknames were handed out. What could have been be more appropriate in this case than Synchro Simon.

Having said this, the word synchro was a marketing term that actually came to the fore towards the end of the development period. Within Bathgate, the gearbox was always referred to as the 3 x 3 because this, in effect, was what it was – a three-speed

Powered by a 47hp three-cylinder Perkins engine, the Leyland 245 was the smallest of the new Synchro models. It was listed at £5643 in March 1978. *© British Motor Industry Heritage Trust*

gearbox with three ranges, designed to provide a total of nine forward ratios plus three in reverse.

Today, over 35 years on, the 3 x 3 might be considered a little old hat. I don't know that for sure because I have to confess to being out of touch with the intricacies of modern-day gearbox specifications. But many aspects of today's tractor design seem to be getting over-complicated, unnecessarily so. I have to wonder whether horsepower for horsepower they are any more productive than they were 30 years or more ago?

What I can say, however, is that throughout the four years of design, development and testing on what were called four-square rig test beds, as well as out in the field, our Leyland prototypes performed like well-disciplined soldiers and rarely put a foot wrong.

The late Bob Beresford placed great faith in the four-square rig as a means of testing. He maintained it had the advantage of being able to be run 24 hours a day, seven days a week, under maximum torque conditions and really racked the mechanicals. For a highly competent engineer, Bob did have some truly non-technical and memorable turns of phrase, some repeatable, others not.

It would have been early 1977 when I first had the opportunity to drive one of the 3 x 3 prototypes, at first within the confines of Bathgate's perimeter roads, then later in the field. As a result of this early experience, I reported back to both Jim Taylor and Bob Turner that the ease of gear-change and general drivability were excellent. I did, however, express some concerns at the choice of ratios, particularly in the medium range. Shortly after voicing my concern, Brian Webb and I were asked to go up to Perthshire where another prototype tractor was at work under the supervision of Marrs of Burrelton, the Leyland distributors in that part of Scotland.

This particular tractor was fitted with a Leyland front-end loader, manufactured by Steel Fabricators of Cardiff. When we arrived it was being used for moving tons of stone and rock and being worked very hard by Gerard Cameron, the son of Mr and Mrs Jim Cameron, the owners of the business. Somewhat reluctantly, Gerard agreed to let us have the tractor to carry out our own field trials.

BELOW LEFT:
A styling mock-up of the Leyland 272 Synchro. It was ultimately rejected as the company simply applied a red stripe on the bonnet decal to distinguish the new models.

BELOW RIGHT:
Leyland's 245 (47hp), 262 (62hp) and 272 (72hp) tractors received the all-new synchromesh gearbox in early 1978.
© *British Motor Industry Heritage Trust*

Brian and I concluded that the ratios weren't exactly what the market-place wanted. On our return to Bathgate we were able to sit down in Ralph Wiggington's office and fine-tune the various achievable combinations. We agreed what the final production version would and should provide in terms of speeds throughout its nine forward ratios.

The four-year development programme was coming to an end, but for those of us in sales and marketing the pace was hotting up. We had a worldwide launch programme to organise, a launch venue had to be agreed and booked, and tractors had to be photographed for the all-important promotional literature. Furthermore, a training programme for our own staff and those of the distributors had to be organised, as well as press releases and photography. Then there was the not inconsiderable task of producing new drivers' handbooks, workshop manuals and parts lists, not just in English but in languages suitable for the world markets where the new Leyland Synchro tractors were to be sold. A busy time, indeed.

By late 1977 preparations for the worldwide launch of the Synchro transmission were gathering pace. Two small episodes spring to mind when recalling these halcyon days of tractor development at Leyland. The first was the reported story surrounding the management's decision to hold the Synchro launch in Torquay. I can, however, only relate the story second-hand as I was not actually party to the discussions.

It was reported that Bob Turner, our powerful and sometimes aggressive sales director, had arranged a meeting with his immediate superior, one Harold Musgrove. Mr Musgrove (people in high authority were always addressed formally in those days) was, in effect, the managing director of the Bathgate factory. Nothing of any great importance happened without his say-so and approval. As I understand it, the meeting had been arranged mainly to discuss the subject of a venue for the launch of the new Synchro tractors.

Bob Turner was determined it should be a high-quality, high-profile event and suggested that the launch should take place in Turkey. In some ways this made sense, because there was a good base there in the form of a British Leyland factory at Izmir (it was still producing a version of the Nuffield 10/60 for Turkey and some surrounding markets).

Now, I am not aware that Mr Musgrove suffered from any form of hearing impediment but, legend has it, he replied that he thought Torquay sounded an excellent idea! Bob Turner passed away several years ago and I doubt if Harold Musgrove is still around so it is unlikely that we shall ever know the truth or otherwise of this story. It did, however, circulate for some time within the confines of the Bathgate factory and, more to the point, it was Torquay and not Turkey that benefited from the experience of a major Leyland product launch.

I can definitely vouch for the truth of the second incident, because I played a part in it. It was always accepted that, as important as the introduction of the Synchro transmission was, there was no requirement from a sales or marketing point of view to change the external styling of the tractor (bonnet shape, etc). Also, it would certainly have been inappropriate to make another colour change so soon after the introduction of the two-tone blue that replaced the Nuffield orange when the new Leyland range was introduced in 1969.

However, I always felt that some outward change was required on the Synchro models, to differentiate them from the old 10-speed types. As a result, it came as a considerable surprise and disappointment to learn that the intention was to do nothing more than fit a small decal, probably no more than 3in x 1in, just forward of the cab with the word Synchro in red. Certainly nothing more inconspicuous could possibly have been devised to advertise the fact that these new tractors were fitted

with what, at the time, was probably the most advanced tractor transmission on the market in that power category.

I was incensed at the thought that our marketing department apparently couldn't comprehend the importance of the new gearbox. So, with the sole knowledge of UK sales manager Jim Taylor, I went to see John James who ran a small commercial art department in the factory.

One evening, when most people had gone home, I drove a demonstration 272 tractor into John's department. We then picked out some red artists tape from his stock and applied two narrow strips, one at the top and one at the bottom of the wide silver decal which surrounded the bonnet of the 10-speed tractors. The tractor was then parked outside the sales office, where it would be seen the following morning by all and sundry as they arrived for the day's work.

At around 8:30am Jim Taylor phoned through to the training school, which was my base, to say he thought the new decal was a great improvement, and that he had asked Bob Turner to make a point of looking at it. However, Bob Beresford, the engineering director, was predictably enraged by what he took to be something of an interference in the responsibilities of his department.

In the final analysis, however, the new decal was accepted. As a result, even 34 years on, it is still possible to tell at a glance whether a Leyland tractor is equipped with a Synchro gearbox or not.

Interestingly, all the tractors featured in the general shots on the new Synchro launch literature were, in fact, 10-speed tractors modified to look like Synchros. This enabled us to start the photography process well in advance of receiving the new tractors from production.

When I describe the Synchro gearbox as probably the most advanced tractor transmission of its time, I am perhaps just a little biased. However, it was very, very good and included some quite novel and advanced design features.

At the Torquay launch, more of which later, it was the joint responsibility of Bob Beresford and Simon Evans to talk about the development, planning and design objectives behind the Synchro. Bob told the assembled dealers that the new transmission was capable of giving a minimum of 5000 trouble-free hours under the most arduous of contracting conditions. It was simple in design, easy to manufacture, yet could still be serviced by relatively unskilled labour.

It would also be necessary to ensure that, within the initial design concepts, there was an ability to make a version completely suitable for torque converter applications, as well as a transmission that would have an on-the-move change capability.

Bob and Simon went on to talk about the strength of the new gearbox casing, the design of the primary input, main shaft and layshaft components, and the size, specification and location of the bearings that supported them. When it came to the subject of synchroniser packs, the heart of any synchromesh-type transmission, the Synchros were enormous compared to those used by International Harvester and David Brown (examples of these were on hand to illustrate the point).

It was, however, not only the size of the synchros that mattered, but also their location. In our case they were positioned on the layshaft, a feature almost unique to

Leyland and one that provided important advantages over the more conventional main shaft situation.

At this point in the presentation things did get quite technical, but the engineering duo knew their stuff and how best to put it across. They stated that it had been found in practice, not only on tractor gearboxes but on automotive units in general, that the synchronising of ratios of more than 4.5:1 was not very successful. To achieve a satisfactory gear spread, tractor ratios were invariably required to exceed this figure.

Synchro packs that were located on the main shaft also had to deal with up to two times more engine torque; in the layshaft position they had to deal with no more than the maximum torque of the power unit.

TOP:
A specially prepared Leyland 272 Synchro leads the Edinburgh Festival Parade along Princes Street in 1978, with George Livingstone at the wheel.

RIGHT:
With its special silver paintwork and Union Jack cab roof, there was certainly no missing the Leyland 272 Synchro that took part in the 1978 Edinburgh Festival.

By this stage in their presentation, Bob and Simon were on a roll, and it was really coming across to the audience that the new transmission was the best thing since sliced bread. Further benefits of the layshaft location came thick and fast, not the least of which were the synchronising times, i.e. the time taken to change gear. Positioning the synchro packs on the layshaft was said to cut shifting times by half, meaning that gear-changes with the new Leyland Synchro transmission were smooth, quick and easy.

What about energy absorption and heat build-up? No problem: the Leyland Synchro packs were completely oil-immersed and heat transfer was therefore superb, unlike some of our competitors.

Superb was the only description for the way in which Bob and Simon did their technical bit in front of the dealers, not once, but probably three or four times, as we all had to do. As things turned out, this was the easy bit: in spite of the fact that it was early spring and we were in Devon, the weather became most unseasonal and did its best to confound our well-laid plans.

In the spring of 1978 the Leyland team was gearing up for the launch of the Synchro transmission. My part in the proceedings began in my office at the tractor training school. At that time the tractor demonstration unit was also based at the school, which adjoined the Bathgate factory, on what was then known as Mosside Farm. I had the joint responsibility for managing both.

A demonstration site for the Synchro launch had been arranged with a farmer close to Torquay, and one of my first tasks was to arrange for the dispatch from Bathgate to Devon of the required quantity of new Synchro tractors. From memory,

Part of the Synchro Drive '79 demonstration fleet, this 262 Synchro is delivering a load of sand in preparation for a floodlit front loader demo the following evening.
© *British Motor Industry Heritage Trust*

I think it had been decided at earlier planning meetings that we would need some-where between nine and 12 of the new 245, 262 and 272 tractors, enough for about four articulated lorry loads. One of these vehicles was our own demonstration unit, driven by its regular driver/demonstrator, Jimmy Lawson, and by Bob Twaddle, who at that time was the demonstration team supervisor.

As Jim and Bob climbed into the truck cab ready for the off it was, I remember, a bright, sunny morning. Not a cloud in the sky but, as usual in Scotland in early February, very cold. If the weather is fine here, I thought, then spring must really be

TOP:
The Synchro Drive '79 programme included product training for dealer salesmen. Alan Hawes, in yellow waterproofs, is pictured with a group of Yorkshire dealers that included staff from Appleyard of Wetherby, Parrish of Scarborough and Robert B. Massey of Market Weighton.
© *British Motor Industry Heritage Trust*

RIGHT:
Floodlit demonstrations of Leyland tractors were a unique feature of the firm's well-attended Synchro Drive '79 tour.
© *British Motor Industry Heritage Trust*

underway in Devon nearly 500 miles to the south. Our convoy of trucks carrying their precious cargo of 12 new Leyland Synchro tractors, some of the very first off the production line, disappeared west along the M8 for the long journey to Torquay.

I had asked Jim and Bob to keep in touch with me and to give regular progress reports (this was, of course, long before the days of the mobile 'phone) and their first call came during a stop at a motorway services somewhere in Gloucestershire. In reply to my question as to progress, Jim replied that the snow was just beginning to settle. Looking out of my office window at the still bright blue skies of southern Scotland, I was sure this was Jim's idea of a joke, but no, Bob Twaddle came on the line to confirm that it was, indeed, snowing and heavily.

The convoy was due to arrive on our Devon farm the following day and it was agreed that we would talk again when the tractors had been off-loaded at the demonstration site. Our venue for a large part of the conference programme, including all the major speeches on the new products, new commercial arrangements and a huge audio-visual presentation, was the prestigious Imperial Hotel right on Torquay's sea front.

Also, to provide covered accommodation on the demonstration site three or four miles away, we had hired a full-size Big Top from Billy Smart's circus. The plan was that distributor principals would have the opportunity to drive the tractors in the circus ring and experience for themselves the easy-changing characteristics of the new Synchro box.

One of the reasons for choosing the south Devon location was that the spring weather would have well and truly arrived by the third week of February. That, at least, was what our Leyland distributors in the area had told us. So, if eggs had not actually hatched then, the hen birds would certainly be sitting on them in nests that had long been built.

Well, I received the next telephone call from Jim and Bob, who confirmed that the tractors had been safely unloaded. That, they said, was the good news. Did I want the bad? The bad news was that overnight the area had experienced one of the heaviest snowfalls ever, with the result that most of the narrow, high-sided Devon lanes around the farm were blocked. As important, if not more so, was the fact that the local fire brigade had been called out to hose the roof of Mr Smart's Big Top, which had been in danger of collapse from the weight of accumulated snow!

Bearing in mind that this new product introduction was planned as a conference for the worldwide distributor network, this unseasonable weather could potentially create major problems. After all, distributor principals and managers would be flying into Heathrow and other international airports from the USA, Australia, New Zealand, South Africa, all parts of Europe and Scandinavia to name but a few. The plan was that they would then be flown down to the local airport at Exeter. However, at this stage, only a few days before the first arrivals were due, the airport was closed with no real prospect of being reopened.

In the event, things did improve from a travel point of view and nobody who had accepted the invitation to attend failed to arrive. In our demonstration fields, however, conditions were far from ideal and a major restructuring of plans had to be put into operation.

Much to the relief of the farmer who had kindly lent us the land, it was agreed that any form of cultivation work was out of the question. It was also decided that many more demonstration-type activities would have to be done under cover and in the relative comfort of the Big Top.

We also decided that we simply had to get some tractors into the conference facility, inside the plushly carpeted surroundings of the Imperial Hotel itself. This decision was easy to make, but much more difficult to implement. Even if the access doors

TOP:
During a demonstration to prove what their new four-wheel drive models could pull, the Leyland team chained a 'dead' two-wheel drive 262 and three-furrow plough behind a four-wheel drive 472 and a four-furrow plough, and pulled away to their hearts' content!
© *British Motor Industry Heritage Trust*

RIGHT:
Leyland's demo driver Ray Runciman makes adjustments as a four-wheel drive 472 prepares to pull a total of seven furrows plus the dead weight of a two-wheel drive 262.
© *British Motor Industry Heritage Trust*

were wide enough, they were certainly not high enough for a Q-cab tractor. The hotel management, while being totally co-operative, pointed out that the area of our presentation stage was over cellars and that the floors were not designed to carry the weight of 72hp agricultural tractors. Lengthy discussions took place and eventually the persuasive powers of Leyland Tractors personnel prevailed.

Bricklayers and carpenters were brought in to make changes to the height of access doors; floors were supported from below with special props; and, to the amazement of some of the few non-Leyland guests, shiny blue tractors were driven into the refined surroundings of their five-star holiday retreat.

Within the conference hall, Leyland distributors were provided with a series of speeches, supported by slick audio-visual presentations covering the development of the new transmission. Delegates were also advised of its new sales features and benefits, how it compared with the competition of the day and how and why it was superior. They also heard about plans for product support following the launch, press advertising campaigns, demonstration support, new literature and product training.

Very soon after the Torquay launch, we were to embark on a country-wide training programme to familiarise service personnel from every UK distributor with the details of the new transmission. Neil Spalding and John Patterson were to implement this. They toured the country in a high-tech, fully-equipped mobile training school, based on a Leyland National bus chassis. It had very few seats, but plenty of standing room and a Synchro box mounted centrally.

In the relative comfort of the Big Top, the demonstration team, supported by Brian Webb and Ray Runciman, with Peter Blair providing a running commentary, put tractors through their paces. Distributor executives from all over the UK and around the world were encouraged to climb into the cabs and experience the easy changing features of the new transmission for themselves.

Leyland's George Livingstone, right, explains the technicalities of the Carraro front axle to a distributor at the 1978 Smithfield Show in London.
© *British Motor Industry Heritage Trust*

Looking back at the whole event, it can safely be said that everybody involved agreed that out of adversity came a huge success. It was very much a team effort and I still maintain that within that Leyland team there was the highest level of professionalism and complete dedication to the range of products that it represented.

New Synchro tractors began to be despatched from the Bathgate factory to markets all over the world in early March 1978. The carefully designed ratios in the new transmission had been well matched to the slow-revving, high-torque characteristics of the 4/98 engine. The result was a combination that enhanced Leyland's reputation for economical high performance in the field. For a time an advertising slogan declaring 'Leyland Tractors are changing gear in 1978' was used and, in modified forms, remained in place for the next few years. This change of gear helped to ensure that production levels at Bathgate stayed at levels rarely exceeded.

TOP:
Two different types of champion photographed on a farm in eastern Scotland during Leyland's Synchro Drive '79 demonstration tour.
© *British Motor Industry Heritage Trust*

RIGHT:
This demonstration unit was specially sign written to mark the introduction of the Leyland Synchro range of tractors in 1978. It covered thousands of miles during the campaigns to promote the new models and was usually driven by Jimmy Lawson.
© *British Motor Industry Heritage Trust*

It is probably still the case today, but back in 1978 the UK was easily one of the most advanced farming nations in terms of its output and general efficiency, when compared to our cousins on the Continent. In spite of this, we were without doubt very slow to grasp the important performance benefits to be gained from the use of smaller, unequal-wheel four-wheel drive tractors.

Certainly, the likes of County, Roadless, Muir-Hill and others had been well ahead of the game at the higher-horsepower end of the market. However, Continental manufacturers and farmers definitely led the way when it came to their acceptance and understanding of the benefits of unequal-wheel, four-wheel drive tractors of up to 80hp.

The potential of four-wheel drive hadn't gone unnoticed at Nuffield: during the late 1950s the firm had four-wheel drive designs in the field undergoing prototype testing. Sadly, by the time I joined the company (1962) the project had been shelved on the basis that there was apparently no demand for four-wheel drive tractors.

Things began to change during the mid-1970s when imported brands such as Same, Fiat, Deutz and Zetor, all of which had been selling four-wheel drive models in their respective home markets for several years, began to make inroads into the UK. The appearance of such makes – yes, there was a time when they were completely unknown in the UK – seemed to prompt Britain's home-based manufacturers to take notice and to do something about it.

A four-wheel drive Leyland 472 Synchro powers away with a Lemken four-furrow plough in the late 1970s. © *British Motor Industry Heritage Trust*

In the case of Leyland it came hard on the heels of the launch of the Synchro gearbox in 1978. So hard, in fact, that only five months later, at the Royal Show of the same year, the 462 and 472 models were introduced. These tractors followed the established and very simple pattern for designating Leyland models: the first digit indicated the number of driven wheels and the following two or three digits the rated engine horsepower.

The 462 and 472 were well executed designs, using an Italian Carraro front axle, providing a very competitive turning circle, together with a centre-mounted, fully-guarded drive shaft. Several manufacturers, including Massey Ferguson, John Deere, IH and, I think, David Brown, came into this sector of the market with, initially, side-mounted drive shafts and all the inherent disadvantages of this arrangement.

The 1978 Royal Show at Stoneleigh was the first occasion that many farmers would have seen the two-wheel drive Synchro models. Coupled with this, we were also exhibiting the new four-wheel drive tractors for the first time. As a result, it was perhaps understandable that the Leyland stand was busier than it had been for several years. In addition to our static display, we also had a demonstration field for the new four-wheel drives just a mile or two from the showground. Farmers and dealers were taken from the stand by minibus to see the 462 and 472 tractors put through their paces.

The field we chose for our demonstration had just had a crop of hay taken from it and was dry and hard on top, and even dryer and harder underneath. To this day I can picture in my mind's eye a Leyland 462 working with a Bomford & Evershed Superflow, and still hear the steady and reassuring note of the 4/98 engine. Proof indeed of the benefits of four-wheel drive combined with a long-stroke, high-torque engine, an excellent set of transmission ratios and a well-engineered four-wheel drive arrangement. The superb 462 sounded for all the world like a well-loaded crawler tractor as it ripped up the dry, solid Warwickshire clay with the Superflow.

During 1978 British Leyland had been in business for just ten years. For the whole of that time the Leyland Tractors operation was a part of what was known as the Truck & Bus Division. In spite of this, the respective paths of the personnel who specialised in trucks and buses rarely crossed ours in the tractor operation. Certainly, there were senior directors who had responsibility for all three products, but it was

generally acknowledged that most of the Truck & Bus personnel knew next to nothing about our product, and we had no interest in theirs.

It came as something of a surprise, therefore, to receive an announcement from Bob Turner that the tractor operation was to get a new marketing manager from within the truck division. One or two individuals had successfully crossed over from tractors into the truck business, but nobody had ever made a success of a move in the opposite direction. What was our respected sales and marketing director thinking of?

I first met our new marketing manager, Les Gumsley, when he came to familiarise himself with what went on within the product training and demonstration departments at Mosside Farm, Bathgate. I think I can say that Les and I talked the same language from the outset. Any fears I may have had that a truck man would not fit into the tractor operation were almost instantly dispelled. Les, apart from his many other strengths, was very much a hands-on promotions man. True enough, one of the first programmes we devised was entitled Synchro Drive '79, the object being to get as many farmers and drivers to test drive the new Synchro models as possible in the shortest possible time.

An ambitious programme of regional demonstration tours was drawn up, the first of these starting in Exeter and finishing six weeks later in Elgin. At the end of that period we calculated that around 2000 potential customers had had hands-on driving experience of our new models. A good start, thought Les, but there must be a better way of doing it. What, he asked, prevented a farmer from attending a professionally organised field demonstration? Many, of course, would be too busy with routine work such as milking, spring work, hay-making or harvesting. We came up with a plan to hold our demonstrations when farmers weren't doing those jobs – like after dark, for instance!

And so the idea of floodlit demonstrations was born, and through late 1979 and into 1980 that's just what we did, a first, probably anywhere in the world. At each of 12 locations, our dealer staff were put through an intensive product training course in the afternoon, while customers were invited to a local hotel in the early evening for a

Replicating Jimmy Saville's flamboyant 'Jim'll Fix It' signature with 72hp Leyland 472 and 272 tractors.

high-tech film and slide presentation. They were then taken by coach to a floodlit field for a full working demonstration followed by a steak sandwich supper. In spite of the complexity of the arrangements, I seem to remember that everything went like clock-work.

The support we received from the implement manufacturers, including Bamfords of Uttoxeter and Colchester Tillage with their Lemken ploughs, was also tremendous. The hard-working Leyland team never missed a trick in their efforts to capitalise on the interest shown by the huge numbers of farmers who attended the demonstrations. It was a job well done.

During 1979 and 1980 the team at Leyland Tractors was kept extremely busy promoting the product range through a series of nation-wide demonstration tours, covering the country from the north to the south and from east to west. One of these demonstrations was held in Sussex. A week or so prior to this particular event I was told that our public relations department had been contacted by the BBC and, in particular, the producers of that popular children's programme, Jim'll Fix It.

The story, as it came through to me, was that two young viewers had written in to ask if Jim could fix it for them to plough with horses. Apparently, this was one thing that Jim couldn't fix, but instead he said he could meet their wish if they would like to plough with real live farm tractors! And so it was that these youngsters, a boy and a girl from different parts of the country, were brought down to our demonstration

The Leyland team responsible for the Jim'll Fix It stunt pose for the camera; top, left to right, me, Martin Stokes and Ray Runciman; bottom, left to right, Ian Jack, Peter Blair and George Livingstone.
© *British Motor Industry Heritage Trust*

site together with the whole panoply of equipment and the huge BBC production team that seems to be so necessary to produce even the simplest of programmes.

Part of the equipment was a huge Simon hydraulic platform which the BBC were going to use to get aerial footage of the action. Ian Jack was given the task of schooling the two youngsters in the art of driving a Leyland 472 fitted with a four-furrow reversible and a Leyland 272 with a three-furrow reversible, both ploughs being Lemkens on loan from the then importer, Colchester Tillage.

All went smoothly and by late morning the BBC's producer declared himself well satisfied with what had been achieved. Then he dropped a bit of a bombshell – he wanted us to plough Jimmy Saville's signature in a nearby grass field!

Those of you who used to watch Jim'll Fix It may recall that Mr Saville's autograph, which always appeared right at the end of the programme, was a particularly rounded and flamboyant affair and the BBC producer expected Ian and I to replicate it with a 72hp tractor and a reversible plough! He could not understand why such a combination could not be driven round almost in circles to write the signature in ploughed turf.

At this stage my discussions with the producer became a little heated, to say the least. I brought them to a close by saying that the best thing for his team would be to retreat to the nearest pub for their lunch while Ian and I would see what we could come up with.

Using electric fencing stakes we marked out, in huge block capitals, the words JIM'LL FIX IT and then ploughed them out. The result was better than we could have hoped for and certainly good enough for the producer on his return from lunch. The Simon platform was brought in to use for high level filming and when the whole thing was broadcast a few weeks later it did look very good. Ian Jack appeared on the programme together with the two youngsters and the closing shots showed the 472 pulling its plough across the bottom of our ploughed message to underline it.

The tractors were, of course, part of the Synchro range. It is worth noting that at the Royal Show of 1979 our new synchromesh transmission was awarded a silver medal by the Royal Agricultural Society of England for its contribution to agriculture.

It seems difficult to comprehend today but back in the late 1970s and early 80s the average size of tractor was still only between 70hp and 80hp. By 1980, however, we were detecting a rise in the national average, nothing major or extreme just minor increases mainly achieved through the growing popularity of engine turbocharging, but an increase nonetheless.

The market plans department within Leyland Tractors forecast that in 1980 sales of two- and four-wheel drive tractors at or around 80hp would account for around 9000 units, making that particular horsepower sector the largest within the UK (compare that with the total size of the market today).

The growing popularity of tractors in the 80hp class temporarily left Leyland at a disadvantage, but not for long. The firm responded brilliantly by adding two further models to its range – the 282 (2WD/82hp) and 482 (4WD/82hp) – at the Royal Smithfield Show in late 1979. The long stroke Leyland 4/98 engine proved to be capable of being turbocharged to provide an additional 10hp.

Turbocharging agricultural tractor engines was still a relatively new science and the design engineers responsible for the development of these new power units left nothing to chance. Since the start of production at Bathgate some 17 years earlier every single engine underwent a period of test bed running. During the development programme of the turbocharged version of the 4/98 series on the Bathgate test beds the new engines were subjected to thermocycling tests. In these, while running at maximum load, they would constantly have the hot coolant water pumped out and cold water pumped in, hour after hour.

Both the Leyland 282 and 482 were fitted with 14 x 34 rear tyres and a hydraulic assistor ram as standard equipment to provide a balanced specification. They quickly became important additions to the range as they achieved better than expected sales both in the UK and many export markets, particularly in Ireland, Europe, Scandinavia, Australia, New Zealand, Canada and the USA.

Their main competitors over 30 years ago, here in the UK and elsewhere, were such tractors as the Ford 6600, the MF 590, the IH 784, the DB 1490, the JD 2140 and the Fiat 780 and Deutz DX85. When we launched the new 282 and 482 models to the UK distributors at a conference in September 1979 at the Birmingham Metropole Hotel we ran through a variety of highly detailed performance and specification comparisons against all our main competitors.

Surprising as it may seem today, in an age where specifications and prices seem to many to have gone right over the top, neither Ford nor MF had synchromesh transmissions anywhere in their ranges and the MF model did not even have an indepen-

'Made in Scotland' was the legend proudly proclaimed by Leyland at the Royal Highland Show in 1979. A full range of Synchro tractors was shown, including the 285, 462 and, taking centre stage, the 272.
© *British Motor Industry Heritage Trust*

dent power take-off. With 215lb/ft of torque and 5200lbs lift at the end of the link arms the 282 Synchro and 482 Synchro models offered superior performance figures in just about every area of their specification.

During the spring of 1980 the Leyland demonstration team embarked upon a second nation-wide programme of flood lit demonstrations, just as we had done a year earlier with the original Synchro models. We had told our dealers and the farming public how good these two new models were, now it was again time to put our money where our mouth was in the field.

The slogan this time was 'Synchro goes Turbo' and by the end of an eight-week demonstration programme on 16 different locations it was calculated that over 5000 farmers and drivers had ploughed and cultivated with the new 282 and 482 models. It was hard work for the Leyland team, but well worth it.

TOP:
Leyland's six-cylinder range never fully lived up to expectations. Later models, including this 85hp 285 working at a 1979 demo, eventually received the Synchro transmission.

LEFT:
Talking shop with David Ebrey and Peter Fogg at the Royal Highland Show in 1979.
© *British Motor Industry Heritage Trust*

Readers of my story will now know that throughout the second half of the 1970s the tractor division of British Leyland benefited from a regular, if not massive, level of investment in product development. All of this helped to ensure that at retail level, where competitors met face to face, Leyland was able at least to hold its own.

Within our own home market I still firmly believe that Leyland tractors were backed by what was probably the best team of people in the agricultural machinery industry. Looking back, the level of commitment and dedication was quite remarkable. So were the standards of knowledge, not only of the product itself, but of its application in the field and of the farming industry into which the tractors were being sold.

It was never really intended that Leyland would ever be market leaders in the tractor business: apart from anything else, production levels at Bathgate could never be sufficiently high to permit such a situation. The factory was designed to produce up to 750 tractors per week, but it is unlikely that this figure was ever achieved. Sadly, as far as I am aware, Bathgate's manufacturing records were either lost or destroyed shortly before the tractor division was sold in late 1981. However, it is a fact that Bathgate regularly produced several hundred tractors a week and more at times of peak demand, particularly in the years following the introduction of the Synchro range.

Massey Ferguson at Coventry and Ford at Basildon could, and did, easily exceed these figures. I think, also, that both David Brown at Meltham and IH at Doncaster were capable of consistently higher production figures and, as a result, could achieve worldwide sales levels in excess of the Scottish-made Leyland range.

Having said all that, the range was immensely popular all over the world and over 70% of production went to meet demand from farmers outside the UK. Within our own home market, however, Scottish farmers together with the Scottish network of Leyland dealers showed a particular loyalty to the locally-built range of tractors. Our market share in Scotland was always considerably higher than the average for the whole of the UK. Many of the dealers had been involved with the product since the days of the Birmingham-built Nuffield, but almost without exception their levels of sales increased as production at the new Bathgate factory came on stream.

In the mid-1960s I had the pleasure of working with most of Nuffield's Scottish dealers and remember with fondness and not a little nostalgia such names as Thomas Corrie at Dumfries and J. & R. Wallace at Castle Douglas. The agricultural machinery section of the former company was managed by John Taylor. Together with Jim Wallace, he did a lot to ensure that there were not many farms in the south-west of Scotland which did not own at least one Bathgate-built tractor.

There was also the Rutherford group of branches in south-east Scotland, and Alex Strang (Tractors) at Portebello, who sold to all three Lothians. Across the Firth of Forth – its road bridge was still under construction when I first began travelling among these dealers – there was Charlie Burnett at Pittenweem, J. B. W. Smith of Cupar and G. & R. Smith at Aberfeldy. Just to the west in Perthshire there was Marrs of Burrelton. I remember this as a company ably, efficiently and attentively run by Mr and Mrs Jim Cameron and their son Gerrard. They achieved their many sales of both Nuffield and Leyland tractors by being mindful of every detail of the needs of their numerous customers, and by providing an excellent level of both technical and parts service.

In the north east, with branches at Forfar, Laurencekirk, Ellon, Elgin and Dingwall, the Leyland range was sold by the Neil Ross group headed up by their very capable, sometimes aggressive and outspoken, but very fair and likeable managing director, Hamish Tocher.

Without exception, all these companies, together with their counterparts south of the border, welcomed the steady flow of new products that came out of Bathgate during the mid and late 1970s. If this was the case in our own home market, it was equally so further afield. My involvement in product planning began in 1978 and the following year I was asked to go to Italy to be present to assist with the launch of the Synchro and four-wheel drive models. This event took place in early March of 1979 and, although it was held in the prestigious grounds of a castle just outside Bologna in the north, dealers from all over that long, narrow country were present. They were eager to learn all they could about the specifications of the new models, which included Synchro versions of the six-cylinder engined 285 and 2100.

I am reliably informed that even today there are in excess of 5000 Nuffield, Leyland and Marshall tractors still at work on farms in Italy. This country is, of course, the home of Fiat, Same, Lamborghini and several other famous marques. For whatever reasons, the UK no longer exports large numbers of tractors to Italy and the balance of tractor trade today is very firmly in the opposite direction.

I happen to know that as a nation the Italians introduced a number of economic measures designed to protect their own tractor industry, not against the import of foreign products, but instead against the sale of those products once they had been imported. For example, the interest rates on the Italian equivalent of our hire purchase loans were considerably lower for machinery that was made in Italy than they were for imported goods.

BELOW LEFT:
'Now hear this! Addressing a crowd of farmers at a public demonstration of Leyland tractors in Scotland in the late 1970s.

BELOW RIGHT:
Leyland Synchro tractors continued to sell well during 1979, while the fact that some competitors had stolen a march with oil immersed brakes, a two-speed PTO and fully live hydraulics hadn't gone unnoticed.
© *British Motor Industry Heritage Trust*

This was, of course, long after the UK had become a member of the European Union and the arrangement was strictly in contravention of all agreements contained within the Treaty of Rome and everything that followed it. But then the Italian law-makers have never played cricket and you have to have a sneaking regard for them because of that. What a pity from the point of view of our now virtually defunct tractor manufacturing industry that our government knew the rudiments of the rules of that noble game and abided by them, rather than seeking to bend them.

Earlier, I recalled how the late 1970s saw the first real signs of a demand for more horsepower from UK farmers, and how at Leyland we introduced turbo-charged versions of the long-stroke 4/98 engine – used in the 282 and 482 models – to meet this demand. From an engineering point of view this was a simple, low-cost exercise and, indeed, the additional 10hp which we knew we needed was achieved fairly easily. Furthermore, we knew that the Bathgate-built 4/98 engine could be called on to give more power as and when the market required it.

Alongside increases in horsepower, another trend began to emerge during the mid to late 1970s. I am referring, of course, to the use of more complicated technology, designs which increasingly used multi-position switches, relays and circuit boards in place of simple hand controls. Whether this was progress or not was debatable, but looking at the specifications of today's tractors the trend has obviously continued. Whether farmers want it or not it would seem to be largely irrelevant as they seem to have little say in the matter.

Was the 1970s trend to increased sophistication led by a demand from the end user, i.e. the farmer, or was it simply the result of novel and inspirational thinking in the design departments of the tractor manufacturers? I have to admit I honestly don't know the answer, although I'm inclined to think it was probably the latter.

I can say without hesitation that it wasn't Leyland who started the trend but, having identified it was there, it obviously couldn't be ignored. So what to do? In fact the product planning pen had been put to paper some years earlier by none other than myself and Les Gumsley, who were given the job of putting some sales and marketing flesh on to the bones of the proposals that had already been drawn up. The results of this work wouldn't be seen for another two years in 1980.

BELOW LEFT:
Synchro and four-wheel drive models were introduced to Italian dealers in March 1979, in the grounds of a castle in Bologna. I am walking out of the picture on the far right.

BELOW RIGHT:
Visitors to the 1979 Highland Show were the first to see the Leyland 285 Synchro. This special show model had a white cab roof and wheels and gold coach lines on its bonnet.
© *British Motor Industry Heritage Trust*

Eight
The End of
the Leyland Era

If you've never worked for a company of the size that British Leyland was in the early 1980s then you're probably fortunate enough not to know the meaning of 'internal politics', 'empire-building' and 'not invented here'! There were ample helpings of all three within what was, at that time, known as the Truck & Bus division, of which Leyland Tractors was a part.

Thirty years and a bit down the line I still have a peculiar sense of loyalty to the company that employed me for just over 20 years, and I find it difficult to tell stories out of school. This is partly out of loyalty and partly because some of those with whom I crossed political swords are sadly no longer with us and therefore not able to give their side of the story. I have been on this earth long enough to know that there are, very often, two sides to every story, both of which can have some strength and validity.

During my time at the Mosside Farm base of the tractor training school there were times when I was required to have one-to-one meetings with foremen and overseers from the production side of the factory. The same applied to managers from departments all over the huge Bathgate complex. It was part of an exercise to develop closer relations between the departments and a better understanding of one another's responsibilities. In my particular case the aim was to give those who were involved in manufacturing and assembly an idea of what was involved in selling the tractor range in the highly competitive world market of the time.

On one occasion the gentleman I was due to see was in charge of a section at the end of the tractor production line, whose responsibility it was to check the completed tractors for their quality of finish, everything from the standard of the paintwork, through to the trim of the quiet cab and the state of the tyres. Complaints from dealers about quality were, in the main, not frequent, but they did happen. This inspector found such criticism rather flippant, not to say unnecessary, and maintained that the odd blemish here or there was of little or no consequence.

The inspector argued that when the tractor arrived at its destination it would be working in conditions far worse than it had experienced on its journey down the production line and through his final inspection area. This man had built himself a little empire at the end of Bathgate's B block and to his way of thinking there was nothing neither it nor he could do that was not right.

I was able to put it to him that what mattered was not his opinion of standards of quality, but how Leyland compared with tractors built in Basildon, Coventry, Meltham and Doncaster, together with those in Germany, France, Italy and elsewhere in the world. Besides, the 272s that he was passing off had a very similar price-tag to the Jaguar cars you used to see in the showroom on Princes Street in Edinburgh. Why should the farmer buying the Jaguar not expect the same quality in the Leyland tractor?

At a rather different level in the spectrum, I also used the analogy of my inspector going into his local Bathgate gardening shop to buy a new spade. Would he accept one that was a little rusty or imperfect in some other way? He reluctantly agreed that he wouldn't.

If this story seems a little trivial, how about political battles at a rather higher level? Yes, they did happen! Fortunately, it wasn't a frequent occurrence, but they did prompt my good colleague Brian Webb to express the view on more than one occasion that it would be more beneficial if we spent more time fighting the competition than we did on political infighting!

All this is quite relevant to a package of product improvement and specification changes that Les Gumsley and I were developing throughout 1978 and 1979 for Leyland's mid-range tractors up to 82hp. Les and I both knew that our tractors could match the competition when it came down to performance in the field. But we could see a situation developing where, surprisingly, this was not sufficient for younger farming customers who, unlike their fathers, had no experience of tractors without such standard creature comforts as power steering, pick-up hitches and quiet cabs with in-cab heating and entertainment. They wanted much more as well. In spite of increased cost implications and the fact that, in the main, there was no benefit in terms of greater performance, some of our rivals were enjoying success with more sophisticated specifications, in some cases at the expense of sales of our beloved Bathgate-built tractors.

Les and I produced a multi-page report for the directors and senior management; this was the way things had to be done, and quite rightly so. The report identified a number of courses of action: at the most pessimistic end was the steady decline in worldwide sales if no product action was taken at all. At the other end of the spectrum were forecasts of increased sales if the company implemented a package of specification and design changes which Les and I considered to be the minimum requirement necessary.

What was really being pointed out to our lords and masters at British Leyland was that by the very late 1970s the Leyland tractor range was not maintaining its competitive edge. Was it Brian Webb (again) who coined the phrase 'The best out-of-date tractor in the world'? Not that such comments would ever be expressed anywhere but within the confines of internal product planning meetings, of course.

What Les and I wanted to see was the timely introduction of four major design changes, together with a lengthy catalogue of detail improvements. We were quite confident that our case was very strong, considering the developing situation in the market place to support our forecasts. However, our report did meet with some pretty strong and aggressive opposition. Most of it emanated from within design and engineering, and in particular from the department director, Bob Beresford. Was this, in part, an example of the 'not invented here' syndrome to which I referred earlier?

At the time it appeared to be very much the case and one or two fairly furious verbal battles took place between Bob on the one side and Les and I on the other. Thirty-five years later it doesn't really matter and, in any case, at top board level our product proposals were received and accepted without any real opposition. Everything that was identified in the report was implemented and in record time, too. The result was the biggest single package of design changes ever implemented by Nuffield or Leyland.

At one fell swoop Leyland customers around the world saw the introduction of a multi-speed PTO, an advanced form of fully live hydraulics and a much improved and strengthened three-point linkage. A new cab option became available at the same time. The basic frame was designed and made in Denmark by Sekura, but all the internal detail was drawn up in Bathgate and it was manufactured by Sekura at Barnsley in the UK. The Explorer, as the new cab was called, did without doubt set new and higher standards of accessibility, vision, comfort and noise levels. For the next few years it kept Leyland abreast of the market leaders in terms of cab design.

And, oh yes, I almost forgot: what about the change to the braking system that Les and I called for in our report? Those of you who are unfamiliar with Nuffield and Leyland tractors may not know that a design of Girling dry disc brakes, introduced for the 10/42 and 10/60 in 1962, remained in production virtually unchanged right through the various model changes up to and including the last of the blue Leyland models.

After a service life of some 13 years, it was not exactly the most efficient system in the world and most manufacturers, although not all, had progressed to an oil-immersed system. That is what Les and I wanted and that is exactly what Bob Beresford and his team in engineering provided us with, and very good it was too.

Leyland's new-look Harvest Gold tractors were introduced in late 1980. The flagship 802/804 models received the new Explorer cab as standard while customers for the 602/604 and 702/704 had two cab options, either the Explorer, left, or economy QM.
© *British Motor Industry Heritage Trust*

With such a wide-ranging package of product change it was deemed logical and desirable to create something of a new image and new identities for our new tractors. Model designations were changed but sensibly continued to give an indication of horse-power and the number of driven wheels. Of even greater significance was the decision to dispense with the two tone blue paintwork that had been part of the world-wide farming scene for more than 10 years. Harvest Gold was to be the new colour and so it was that the new Bathgate-built tractors became known as the Harvest Gold range.

In much the same way as the specification and colour changes outlined had a dramatic and far-reaching effect on the competitive standing of the Leyland range of tractors, so they also did on certain members of the Leyland team.

The Harvest Gold range was launched to the world in late 1980 and it so happened that the late 1970s and early 80s were, within the massive conglomerate that was British Leyland, a time of great change and reorganisation.

The Truck & Bus division, of which Leyland's tractor division was a part, was included in this restructuring. More to the point, as far as I was concerned, the tractor training and demonstration centre based at Mosside Farm, Bathgate, now came under a centralised management regime based in Leyland, Lancashire. It was to be headed by a specialist general training manager, whose knowledge of trucks and buses was probably first class, but of tractors and all things agricultural was little better than nil.

The prospect of becoming part of a set-up not 100% dedicated to tractors did not appeal to me, so I declined the opportunity to stay at Mosside Farm. Les Gumsley had already indicated that he wanted me to continue to be part of his sales and mar-keting team and this appealed to me, even though it involved relocating my family to Lancashire.

By the middle of 1979 we had sold our bungalow near Selkirk in the delightful Scottish Borders and moved south to a new home just a few miles outside Preston. This was a convenient location because part of the reorganisation involved moving

BELOW LEFT:
The new Explorer cab was designed by Sekura in Denmark, with input from Leyland.
© *British Motor Industry Heritage Trust*

BELOW RIGHT:
A Leyland 702 equipped with the Explorer cab option. Power came from a four-cylinder Leyland 4/98 engine with a rating of 72hp.
© *British Motor Industry Heritage Trust*

the Truck & Bus division's entire sales, service and marketing departments into a multi-storey office block in the middle of the town, known as the Guild Centre. Leyland tractor operations occupied the entire 6th floor of this building.

Following this move, and for a period of six months or so thereafter, my job responsibilities did not change dramatically, apart from the fact that I no longer had any involvement in the management of product training or demonstrations. As far as the former was concerned this became the responsibility of John Paterson, who had been a long-standing and very capable member of the training team at Mosside Farm. I continued to work alongside Les Gumsley and, with the title of UK marketing manager, saw the Harvest Gold product development package through the final stages of its progress into production.

At around this time the reorganisation programme involved even more truck personnel becoming involved in tractors; it was almost as though the tractor operation was being used as a depository for surplus personnel from other divisions. Matters came to something of a head when one of the truck team was appointed general marketing manager of the tractor division. It proved to be something of a watershed, because it was an appointment that Les Gumsley found very difficult to accept.

I knew at the time that Les was being head-hunted by Fiat Agriculture in the UK, whose headquarters at the time were in Bury St Edmunds. With this latest appointment he decided that the time was now right for him to make the move. Throughout his time working in Leyland's tractor division Les came to be regarded as a first class marketing and promotions man. Without doubt Leyland's loss was Fiat's gain.

While it could not be said that everything was in a state of complete flux, many aspects of the management set-up were subject to change. By this time Bob Turner had sadly moved on and had been replaced by a new tractor supremo, Steve Herrick. Right at the top of the Truck & Bus division tree was Frank Andrew, who had previously worked for the company in Australia.

BELOW LEFT:
To mark the launch of the Golden Harvest range of tractors, a nationwide series of dealer evenings was organized. Here I am installing a Leyland tie during an open evening at J. B. W. Smith's dealership at Cupar in Fife.

BELOW RIGHT:
Leyland's 602 and 604 tractors were available with a choice of cabs, either the economy QM, seen here, or the optional Sekura-built Explorer.
© *British Motor Industry Heritage Trust*

Ever since the introduction of the Nuffield Universal in 1948, Australia had been and still was a major export market for Leyland. Because of this Frank had a good working knowledge of the product and the tractor market. Those of us whose working life was tractors felt this could only be to the advantage of the product in the future.

One of Steve Herrick's first moves was to appoint Keir Wyatt, an established member of the service team, to the position of UK sales and service manager. David Ebrey had particular responsibility for technical service in this new structure, in which the UK was divided into three regions for the more effective management of sales. Ray Runciman had sales responsibility for the southern most of the three, Brian Webb for the Midlands and I was given the same responsibility for the north of England, Scotland and Northern Ireland. Each of the three regional managers also had two area managers and, in my case, these were Ian Jack and Roy Harling; I also had the good fortune to have the support and backing of Andy McMeechan covering the whole of the northern region as service engineer.

So it was that a new brush was in place in the early part of 1980 to prepare the path for the introduction of the new Harvest Gold range of Leyland tractors. Some of the bristles of the new brush were, in my view, too new to the tractor business and too steeped in products that didn't have two smaller wheels at the front and two larger ones at the back. They were lacking in dedication and failed to capitalise on the opportunities that were being offered by the wide-ranging package of design and specification changes that had been built into the new range. That was my opinion then and I have to say that my view has not mellowed much with the passing of 30 years and more.

Be that as it may, the public introduction of the Harvest Gold range was timed for the Royal Smithfield Show of 1980. This was preceded, in early November, by launches to the distributors and dealers, and separately for the gentlemen of the agricultural press.

There was a time when I held a number of the members of this latter group in not very high esteem. Clearly, they were at liberty to form their own opinions of what they were being introduced to by the manufacturers and to comment in their columns accordingly.

At the launch, in spite of a lengthy list of technical changes, if not innovations, to which one reporter could have devoted more of his valuable column inches, he could not avoid the temptation to be sarcastic about the new colour scheme and comment that it was more like calf scour yellow than Harvest Gold! Would he, I wonder, have had the temerity to describe John Deere's colour as silage slurry green or that of MF as rotten tomato red? I think not.

At that time Leyland's Truck & Bus division was achieving a total sales turnover of something in excess of £500mn. In his address at the launch Frank Andrew made it plain that Leyland's tractor division accounted for over 10% of that figure. Importantly, it contributed to the profitability of the division by a far greater percentage than that.

What he may not have stressed, and any omission in those days would not have been picked up on simply because it was taken as read, could have been the proportion of total sales beyond our shores. This is not to forget that 30 years ago the UK was still a major exporter of tractors. With Leyland it was usually the case that at least 80% of each year's production would now be exported. Together with virtually the whole of the UK agricultural manufacturing industry, Leyland tractors would make a valuable contribution to the nation's balance of payments. Sadly, the situation is very different today.

I have already drawn attention to the new management structure that found its way into the Leyland tractor operation on the 6th floor of the Guild Centre, Preston, just prior to the introduction of the Harvest Gold range.

The range itself was full of new features that were eminently capable of being demonstrated in the field to very good effect. Sadly, the new marketing regime appeared not to appreciate this and made no meaningful plans to implement a repeat of the demonstration programme we had carried out so successfully during the late 1970s. Back then we made a very good fist of promoting the new Synchro models followed, a short time later, by the four-wheel drive 462 and 472 and their turbo-charged counterparts, the 282 and 482.

Certainly, these promotions had not been low-cost affairs to put on the road, but in terms of cost effectiveness they were very worthwhile. Importantly, they focused the attention of thousands of customers across the country, many of whom were farming with rival brands. Many of our distributors and dealers were able to convert the interest generated into firm sales. Reports of each and every sale were welcomed and recorded in order to assess the effectiveness of each demonstration. Deals that took out a competitive make – conquest sales – were always the ones that gave rise to the greatest sense of achievement and satisfaction.

However, in the early part of 1981 there was an absence of the promotional planning that was needed to capitalise on the considerable interest shown in the new Harvest Gold products at their first public outing at the Royal Smithfield Show the previous December. We had what was possibly the best cab in the business, a new multi-speed PTO and fully live hydraulics with the selectable flow rates up to a maximum of 12.1gal/min for external services. This combination was more than a match for any of the competition at the time. Importantly for existing Leyland owners, we had come abreast of the competition with the introduction of multi-disc oil-immersed brakes, something that Leyland users around the world had been requesting for a long time.

We did, of course, get our products into the market place if not, initially, into the fields for demonstrations. I remember how, together with Ian Jack, Roy Harling and Andy McMeechan, I spent many evenings supporting distributors who had been encouraged to organise open events on their premises. The prospect of being able to see the models on their door-step appealed to local farmers and attendances were generally very good. However, it wasn't quite the same as the floodlit demonstrations from the late 1970s.

I suppose it's not pleasant to look back at failure or disappointment. The almost unrecorded demise of the six-cylinder 285 and 2100 models fell into one or other of these categories, depending upon your experiences with them. Certainly, they didn't continue long enough to be given the coat of Harvest Gold paint which transformed the appearance of their four-cylinder counterparts.

The fact is that they were quietly dropped from production and from the Leyland range during 1979. Out in the market place this didn't cause any real surprise. Within the Bathgate factory, however, and particularly within the engineering department, there was some disillusionment.

A programme had been in hand for some time with the aim of developing a 100hp tractor which, unlike the County-based 485 and 4100 models, with their equal-sized wheels front and rear, had smaller wheels at the front and used a heavier-duty Carraro axle than that fitted to the four-cylinder four-wheel drives. This tractor would have had a version of the new Explorer cab made in Denmark by Sekura and the early prototype began to develop a very promising appearance.

Who, at that time, could have forecast what the future would have held for this tractor had its development been completed and it had gone into production? The market was heading strongly in the general direction of higher horsepower tractors and the trend towards four-wheel drive was firmly established. Perhaps the reason for the cancellation of the programme was already known to a select number of senior directors within Leyland's tractor operations and the Truck & Bus division. I certainly believe that it was and the reason was neither technical nor mechanical.

Another model that experienced a very quiet demise was the 25hp Leyland 154. Born out of the original BMC Mini tractor and the Nuffield 4/25, the 154 never enjoyed spectacular sales, but it was always a popular choice in the turf and sports ground maintenance market. In the early days it had a virtual monopoly in this sector, until the likes of the Japanese-built Kubota and Iseki models began to make an appearance in this country.

The early versions of these imported tractors were almost exclusively four-wheel drive and many would argue that they needed to be. The two-wheel drive Nuffield 4/25 and Leyland 154 were more than their match in the field, but the fact that the foreigners came with four-wheel drive as standard gave them, on paper, a degree of specification superiority.

As a result they made considerable inroads into a market where, for several years, the Nuffield 4/25 and Leyland 154 had reigned almost supreme.

During 1979 a decision was taken to transfer production of the Leyland 154 from Bathgate to a company in Turkey, which was part owned by British Leyland and based in Izmir. Anything that affected production levels and therefore employment at Bathgate was, as a matter of course, discussed with the unions and there was a degree of understandable concern on their part at the loss of this particular product. The transfer of 154 production to Turkey was, therefore, made on the understanding that the Izmir-built product would not be imported into the UK. There was a twist to this story because Turkish-built tractors did, in fact, come to this country.

The Turkish factory introduced an improved model, the Leyland 302, based around a larger 1.8-litre indirect diesel engine rated at 30hp. This model also had a redesigned bonnet which gave it a strong family resemblance to the new Harvest Gold mid-range models, a stronger front axle, increased hydraulic lift capacity and a larger fuel tank and hydraulic oil reservoir.

The 302 models came into the UK in semi-kit form and were built up and distributed from a Leyland depot just to the north of London, where Ray Runciman had

TOP:
Listening to what Charlie Burnett, right, has to say during an open evening held by Leyland dealer Burnett's of Pittenweem in Fife in early 1981.

LEFT:
Powered by a lively four-cylinder turbo engine that produced 82hp, the top-of-the-range Leyland 804 was capable of pulling a four-furrow reversible plough.
© *British Motor Industry Heritage Trust*

his regional sales office. Ray, with his first class technical knowledge of tractors in general, was also able to oversee the installation of a very good OECD approved Q cab.

So, was there any significance in the fact that during 1979 the tractor factory at Bathgate had ceased the production of its six-cylinder tractors and had seen the smallest model in the range leave for Turkey, together with all its specialised machine tools?

Perhaps because the 154 and 285, 485, 2100 and 4100 models were comparatively low-volume products, not many people attached much importance to the matter? Perhaps they were so involved in promoting the sale of the Harvest Gold range that they were too busy to notice. Perhaps some of them were just not in the right place at the right time?

Talking about times and places, it just so happened that my regional sales office on the 6th floor of the Guild Centre was right next door to Steve Herrick, our new sales director, and opposite that of Keir Wyatt, the recently appointed sales and service manager. From where I sat, frequently with a telephone glued to my ear, I had a good view of the various comings and goings through the large general office, and in particular those that were in the direction of Steve and Keir's offices.

From roughly the middle of 1981 it became noticeable that more and more meetings were being held behind the normally open doors of these two offices. Nothing very unusual about that, you might say, for this was a busy international sales environment. But the doors were invariably now closed to the outside world – most strange.

Moreover, with increasing frequency the same faces from somewhere outside the company would arrive to attend these meetings. Something, as the saying goes, seemed to be going on. Occasionally I would be asked by my colleagues, who had desks in the general office, what I knew about Track Marshall and did the name Nickerson mean anything to me? Well, of course, both names were known to me, so perhaps something was, indeed, going on.

Two sets of brochures were produced for the Leyland Harvest Gold tractors; one for European markets, where cabs were a legal requirement, and one for developing markets, where an open platform or sun shade would usually suffice.
© *British Motor Industry Heritage Trust*

THE HARVEST GOLD RANGE

	502	602/604	702/704	802/804
Engine	Perkins	Leyland	Leyland	Leyland
Cylinders	3	4	4	4 turbo
Horsepower	47	62	72	82
Cab	QM	QM/Explorer	QM/Explorer	Explorer
Transmission	9F/3R	9F/3R	9F/3R	9F/3R

Nine
Moving to Marshall

Living in the 21st century, most people now accept that a job for life is largely a thing of the past, although happily it may still apply in some areas of the farming industry. Outside farming, in our declining manufacturing industries and in the workshops of this green and still very pleasant land, long-term job security has become increasingly harder to find.

Back in 1981 most of Leyland's tractor sales team had been working with the product for around 20 years. For people like Brian Webb, Ray Runciman, Martin Stokes, Andy McMeechan and myself, job complacency was never an issue: we were dedicated to the cause and cared passionately about the product. On the other hand, there seemed to be no reason to be concerned about our future. And, in any case, most of us were always far too busy to give such matters much, if any thought. In hindsight how naive we all were.

However, as I have already mentioned, during the latter half of 1981 the names Track Marshall, Charles Nickerson and Gainsborough began to be mentioned with increasing frequency in the hub of Leyland's busy sales, marketing and service operation, located on the sixth floor of the Guild Centre in Preston.

Some years earlier, the same Charles Nickerson had acquired the Track Marshall business from British Leyland's Special Products Division. The argument thereby followed that he probably still had good contacts within British Leyland. To most of us, it seemed inconceivable that Leyland's Truck & Bus division would wish to divest itself or, to put it crudely, get rid of the Leyland tractor range. After all, at the time, the new and vastly improved Harvest Gold tractors were less than 12 months old.

Tractors accounted for a significant proportion of the Bathgate plant's total production. What would happen to C block at Bathgate without the tractor range?

One theory that came to be bandied about at the time was a proposed transfer of the Land-Rover assembly line to Bathgate, a move that would have increased production levels to over and above those being achieved in British Leyland's Midlands plant.

To their credit, management within the tractor division and at higher levels within the Truck & Bus division didn't prolong the speculation and uncertainty that had, inevitably, been generated by the rumours.

The company announced its plans at a huge internal conference sometime in the late summer of 1981. Virtually all the sales, marketing and service personnel from Truck & Bus heard the company's senior directors detail some of their plans for the immediate and longer term future of the division. As far as we in tractors were concerned it was confirmed that our division was to be disposed of and, yes, the purchaser would be Charles Nickerson, a Lincolnshire farm and the owner of the Track Marshall company in Gainsborough.

Looking back, it can be said that Leyland's tractor division had the rather dubious honour of being the first part of the massive British Leyland conglomerate to be privatised. Doubtless, while the prime minister of the time, Margaret Thatcher, reigned supreme, it would not be the last and along with the coal mining industry she

RIGHT:
Bathgate's first Nuffield 342 rolled off the line in 1962. Eric Hopkins, front row in white coat, followed production from Birmingham to Bathgate then finally, in 1982, to Gainsborough.
© *British Motor Industry Heritage Trust*

BELOW:
Marshall's sprawling Britannia Works, shown here in the 1870s, covered a vast area in the centre of Gainsborough in Lincolnshire.

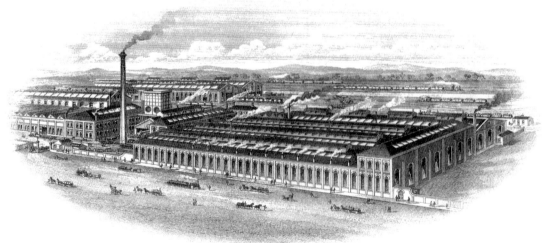

BOILER DEPARTMENT   BRITANNIA WORKS

and her government appeared to have no compunction about throwing production, exports and employment to the dogs and into the ever-welcoming and open arms of overseas competitors.

What of the Bathgate plant? What of the future of the massive plant that only 20 years before had begun to produce the first of a long line of trucks, diesel engines and tractors? In spite of the speculation, it seemed there were no plans to transfer the production of Land-Rovers into the space in C block that would be left vacant when the tractor division moved out. Oddly, it seemed that there were absolutely no plans to do anything with the shortly to be empty tractor production facility. If C block could be left empty, the question had to be asked what chances for the future of A, B, D and E blocks, and all the jobs contained within them?

Along with privatisation came rationalisation, retraction and massive redundancies. That was the name of the game in early 1980s Britain. The huge Bathgate site, which in its heyday provided up to 6000 jobs and produced many millions of pounds for the economy, closed completely in 1986 and is now a housing estate.

In just over 25 years the factory that started life as BMC Scotland was opened, closed down and then knocked down. This was no Far East sweat shop operation; in 1962 it was a state-of-the-art design and production facility covering 260 acres, of which 110 were developed.

C block, where the first Nuffield and then Leyland tractors were produced, covered 244,800sq ft; B block, which produced both four- and six-cylinder engines for trucks and tractors, covered 694,800sq ft. It also housed many of Bathgate's 3400 machine tools and was at the time almost certainly the largest machine shop in Europe.

Bathgate had a total covered area of 1.5mn sq ft, five miles of internal roads, four miles of internal railways, seven assembly tracks, two paint plants, one engine test unit and one heat treatment facility.

Marshall's first wheeled tractor spell ended in disappointment in 1960 after sales of the six-cylinder MP6 failed to live up to expectations.

129

Sadly, no precise record of total tractor production exists today. I would estimate, however, that several hundred thousand tractors went out through those swinging doors at the end of the C block production line. Something in the region of 70% of them would have been exported to markets all over the world.

Bathgate was by no means the largest of the UK's tractor producing factories. However, it made a significant contribution to the fact that, as a nation, we once used to export more tractors than the rest of the world combined. Present day performance in this respect hardly makes a mark on the statistician's sheet of graph paper.

The very first tractor, a Nuffield 342, came off the production line during the first half of 1962. It was assembled, as were the first dozen or so tractors, from kits of parts produced in the first Nuffield factory at Ward End, Birmingham, where production of the larger 460 continued for a short time.

This early assembly process was over-seen by a young Birmingham man called Eric Hopkins. Eric had been involved in production at Ward End and moved north to Bathgate to help get the wheels of production moving. After the sale of Leyland's tractor division to Charles Nickerson and the closure of C block, he moved south again. Throughout 1982 and beyond he played a significant part in getting production under way in our new home in the old Marshall factory in Gainsborough.

As far as I can recall Eric is the only person to have been involved in manufacturing at all three factories – Birmingham, Bathgate and Gainsborough. Whether or not Eric himself, who is now living back in Scotland, close to Bathgate, is aware of this fact I am not sure. However, for those with a close interest in the history of the Nuffield, Leyland and Marshall brands, it is a noteworthy achievement.

Also worthy of note, as a new chapter began to open in the history of the Leyland tractor, was the fact that its new home in Gainsborough was, unlike Bathgate,

Having saved Track Marshall from oblivion in 1979, Lincolnshire farmer Charles Nickerson took on the much stiffer challenge of transferring Leyland production from Bathgate to Gainsborough in 1982.
Photo: Bill King

steeped in history. Marshall's Britannia Works in the centre of Gainsborough was established not in the 1900s but in the 1800s – 1848 to be precise.

The new home of the Leyland tractor range was the old Marshall factory in Gainsborough, north Lincolnshire. Living as I still do very close to this old market town, I am well aware of people still living locally who are far more familiar with the history of the famous Marshall company.

There are still people in Gainsborough who worked for the company when the world-famous single-cylinder Field Marshalls were developed and produced. By virtue of the fact they worked in the place, they have accumulated a wealth of first-hand knowledge about the company, its products, its people and personalities. Fortunately, much of this history has been collated and documented by various authors over the years.

I think I am correct in saying that the company started trading in 1848 and produced its first portable steam engine in 1856. Growth came quickly and by 1870 the firm employed a workforce of 550 and occupied a 4.5-acre site in the centre of the town. Products included a range of farm implements, boilers and tea-processing machinery.

TOP:
A precious cargo of Leyland Harvest Gold tractors passes through the Lincolnshire countryside en-route to Gainsborough.

LEFT:
The first train-load of Bathgate-built Leyland tractors reaches its journey's end, the sidings at the rear of Marshall's Britannia Works factory in Gainsborough.

Around this time the range of steam engines was being expanded, including such types as vertical, horizontal, single, double and compound. By 1892 Marshall factories in the town covered 20 acres and employed 2200 people.

In 1909 the firm produced its first crude oil-engined agricultural tractors. The Colonial tractors were so called because they were designed and destined for work in Australia and Canada. By the following year the Britannia and Trent Works in Gainsborough occupied 39 acres and provided employment for 4000 of the town's residents.

Russia became a major market for boilers and in 1925 Marshall exported 140 steam rollers to Greece. In 1930 production of the single-cylinder 15/30 diesel tractor began, followed in 1936 by the introduction of the model M. During the Second World War much of the factory was turned over to the production of armaments, which included heavy gun mountings and midget submarines.

Marshall celebrated its centenary in 1948, incidentally the same year that the Nuffield Universal tractor was introduced to world markets, and launched the Fowler VF crawler.

Production levels of the famous series of single-cylinder Field Marshall wheeled tractors were dramatically increased to meet post-war demand. This was followed in 1956 by the introduction of the Track Marshall marque and the six-cylinder-engined MP6 wheeled tractor. As for the latter, records show that as few as 200 were produced, the majority for export.

In 1975 the company was acquired by British Leyland, becoming part of its Special Products Division. British Leyland already owned Grantham-based Aveling Barford and the two companies were merged under the umbrella name Aveling Marshall Ltd. Four years later part of the Gainsborough factory was brought into private ownership, by Charles Nickerson, renamed Track Marshall Ltd and streamlined so that Track Marshall crawlers became its primary product.

The buffer stock of built-up tractors, pictured on arrival at the Britannia Works in Gainsborough in February 1982, gave Marshall something to sell while it completed the installation of its own assembly line.

This is a potted history of Marshall which, for well over a century, was very much a major part of the life and work of the small town of Gainsborough. The firm was the town's largest employer and for many years the social and commercial fortunes of the two were inextricably linked.

By the early 1980s, however, Marshall was considerably smaller than it had been in its heyday. Nevertheless it was into this background of large scale engineering excellence, a worldwide reputation and the closest of connections with farming that the Leyland range of tractors was about to be thrust.

TOP:
Leyland sales and service personnel who helped to transfer the tractor division to Marshall included, from left: Bob Twaddle (remained with Leyland), David Ebrey (service manager), Julian Bown (service), Richmond Leeson (demo supervisor), Ron Kettle (export sales), me (regional sales manager), Alan Hawes (regional sales manager), John Mill (service engineer) and Mike Barnes (design manager).

LEFT:
This aerial view of Marshall's Britannia Works factory in Gainsborough was taken in 1982 or 1983, not long after the arrival of the Bathgate-built Harvest Gold tractors.

It wasn't just the range of tractors that faced a considerable move: numbers of long-serving, dedicated and experienced staff were also invited to join Marshall in Gainsborough. It is a well-known fact that not all the individuals involved agreed with the commercial decisions made within British Leyland, or the political decisions made somewhere close to Downing Street that brought the move about.

TOP:
The proud tractor legacy of Marshall, Sons & Co included the single-cylinder model M tractor produced from 1936 to 1945.

RIGHT:
Marshall had this Colonial oil tractor shipped back from Australia and restored for its museum at Gainsborough. It now belongs to Robert Crawford of Frithville, Boston.

As it transpired, nobody was actually forced to make the move to Gainsborough. Everyone in sales and marketing was interviewed by the directors of Marshall, the interviews taking place very informally in one of the boardrooms at the Guild Centre in Preston. Before the end of the day most members of staff knew whether or not they were wanted by the Marshall organisation.

It had been clear for some time that the size of the Marshall operation was such that not everybody could or would be offered employment. As the day progressed we began to realise that we were witnessing the break-up of one of the most knowledge-able and dedicated organisations anywhere in the world – that was how good I believed (and still believe) the Leyland tractor division really was. It was a very sad day in more ways than one, even for those of us with a job to go to in Gainsborough.

Particularly difficult to accept was the fact that people you knew and had worked closely with were not going to be there in the future. These were people whose knowl-edge of the entire tractor range, its strengths and its weaknesses, its applications in the field, and general knowledge of farming methods, was second to none and irreplacea-ble. In the case of several, they would gladly be snapped up by some of our competitors.

Some of the most notable and surprising exclusions from the list included Ian Jack, Martin Stokes and Brian Webb, and from export sales there was Peter Hitchings who, together with several members of export service, had travelled the world in support of the product range.

Export trips were never the glamorous experiences many people think them to be. In some cases they were downright unpleasant and dangerous. Think of Angola, the Sudan, Egypt and Israel, together with some South American countries, but tractors were being sold there and they and the companies selling them had to be supported.

In spite of what I have just said, the list of people offered jobs by Marshall was a long one. One of my photographs shows several of us and happily there were many more, including a number from the factory floor areas in Bathgate.

John Coull came south to head up the final inspection department; Pat Mac-Namarra was employed to supervise transmission assembly; and Rob Mackie was a production foreman.

Then, of course, there was Eric Hopkins, who started his working life at the original Nuffield factory in Birmingham, moved to Bathgate when it opened in 1961/62 and then came to Gainsborough as production manager.

Those of us who were offered and accepted positions in Gainsborough finished our employment with British Leyland on the last working day of February 1982 and began working for Marshall on the first day of March – it was as quick as that.

Not so, I suspect, the actual sale and transfer of ownership of the business. Very few people will know when discussions first took place between the two companies, how long the negotiations went on for, or what the purchase price was. The discus-sions must have been complicated, bearing in mind the complexities of the deal, which had to include everything necessary to permit the earliest possible start of tractor manufacture in Gainsborough. Machine tools, both large and small, unsold tractor stocks, production components and spare parts all had to be moved from Bathgate to Gainsborough, a distance of about 300 miles.

Thinking back, I am now almost convinced that the introduction of the Harvest Gold range of Leyland tractors was sanctioned by Bathgate's ruling powers for only one reason. The decision either to close the business or to try to sell it had been taken some years earlier, when Les Gumsley and I were driving the new specification requirements through the product planning system at Bathgate.

The point I'm driving at is this: the Harvest Gold tractor range was a much more saleable commodity than the old Synchro range. If my intuition is right, the possibility of ceasing tractor production at Bathgate or selling off the tractor business would have been on confidential board meeting agendas as long ago as 1978. In any event, it was closure as far as most of the employees and their families at Bathgate were concerned. Not so for the people of Gainsborough, for whom the sale of the Leyland tractor division to Marshall created some much-needed employment opportunities.

The existing Track Marshall business occupied only about a quarter of the total company site and employed probably no more than 50 people. The rest of the site was large enough to accept a somewhat scaled-down and much-changed version of Bathgate's production facilities. There was also an ample supply of the right people to staff the business during its move from Scotland and supervise the tractor division's installation in its new home, and to work in the plant when production was up and running.

For those of us who had moved from Leyland it was, for several months, no longer a case of suit and tie, office desk and secretary. Instead, it was a real roll-up-your-sleeves job as we got to grips with the mountains of spare parts and components that arrived daily from Bathgate and Leyland's parts operation in Cowley.

Several train-loads of tractors were backed into the rail sidings that ran down the eastern perimeter of the factory and these all had to be unloaded and driven away to secure storage areas. And so it went on, although everything was done with enthusiasm and goodwill. The tractor range which had been part of our working lives for 20 or more years was in good hands, and there was a determination to get it back in production and on sale to world markets as soon as possible.

Not many factory buildings in this country, or for that matter anywhere else in the developed world, were designed to make the very maximum use of every square inch of the area of land on which they were built.

BELOW LEFT:
These four tractors were the first of the buffer stock of Bathgate-built tractors to be rebadged as Marshalls at Gainsborough in 1982. They were also subjected to a rigorous quality inspection.

BELOW RIGHT:
Production of the first Gainsborough-built Marshall in the autumn of 1982 was a joyous occasion for company chairman Charles Nickerson, right, and sales director Kier Wyatt.

Marshall's Britannia Works, located close to the centre of the Lincolnshire town of Gainsborough, was different. Its long, brick frontage came right up to the pedestrian footpath on Beaumont Street as it snaked its way northwards through the town, faithfully following every curve and meander of the town's main thoroughfare.

A very high proportion of the huge factory complex was built from brick, each one made from clay excavated when the steeply sloping site between Beaumont Street and the parallel railway line was leveled when the factory was built in the 19th century. Only recently has much of the complex been demolished, partly to make way for yet another supermarket and, further along Beaumont Street, the impressive and tasteful architecture of the Marshall's Yard complex of smaller shop units.

What a tragedy that so much of British manufacturing is now represented only in museums. It is certainly good to recognise and remember our heritage, but what an inheritance for the generations of would-be craftsmen and young job seekers.

When the Marshall factory was demolished a few years ago, an entrepreneurial shopkeeper in Gainsborough acquired a quantity of bricks from the Marshall site and was selling them for £1 apiece. Each one is embossed with the inscription M. S. & Co, short for Marshall, Sons & Co. For some of us who worked there the purchase of one or two bricks was an absolute must.

However, enough of my sanctimonious lamentations about present-day Gainsborough. Let's go back to early 1982 when the southern half of the Britannia Works was very definitely alive with activity. When those of us from the Leyland centres of Bathgate and Preston first saw our new base much of it was in a semi-derelict condition. The first thoughts of many were 'Is it going to work?' and 'How long is it going to take to get the wheels of production turning?'.

This view of Britannia Works was taken in 1982, not long after Marshall took delivery of a stock of tractors from Leyland. Chairman Charles Nickerson and works manager Harold Clarke's office can be seen in the foreground, while tractor assembly was undertaken in the brick buildings in the background.

Many of the factory floor areas designated for production of the old Leyland range of tractors were strewn with hundreds of tons of part-finished components, storage bins and general scrap which just lay where it had been left by the previous owners of the plant. All this had to be cleared and disposed of before the buildings themselves could be cleaned down. A start could then be made on installing the machine tools that had come down from Bathgate and the establishment of production lines.

The clearance task was mammoth in its proportions. Thankfully, the whole move had been well thought out, with the result that it was almost possible to see a daily improvement in how the whole thing would appear on completion, and the more we saw, the more we were impressed.

The production area certainly wasn't a second Bathgate, and never would be, but a totally workable tractor production facility appeared to be in the making. It transpired that tractor assembly would be carried out in two separate but adjoining areas of the factory. The first area was designated for the assembly of the engine, clutch, gearbox, front and rear axles and hydraulics – basically the whole skid unit – which was also painted in the same area. These skid units were then transferred to an overhead conveyor system to be carried into the second area, where they were fitted with one of two types of cab, electrics, panels, wheels and tyres, etc.

At Bathgate most of these operations were carried out on one long conventional production line but, as time would tell, the Gainsborough system, while definitely not having the same output in terms of overall capacity, was just as capable of producing good tractors.

BELOW LEFT:
An overhead conveyor system transported the completed Marshall skid units from the initial assembly area through to the trim and cab shop.

BELOW RIGHT:
Part of what would eventually become the finishing shop for Marshall wheeled tractors, as first seen by the ex-Leyland team in February 1982.

However, in early 1982 the achievement of much of what I have just described was still several months away in terms of being put into practice. It wasn't just the production levels where Gainsborough differed to Bathgate. For those of us who had come from Leyland and in particular for people like myself who had been based at the Scottish factory, the man management system was totally different. In fact it was much better.

In the early days the way the plant was managed was effective and worked well. The board of the company, including chairman Charles Nickerson, was much closer to its workforce and less aloof than had been the case at British Leyland.

Charles Nickerson was approachable and would listen with interest to what most of his staff had to say. This included not just the white collar members of his workforce, but also those employed on the production line, in the parts department or in any other capacity.

Mr Nickerson regularly walked through the various production and assembly areas, stopping to talk to individuals, presumably about what their particular task happened to be that day. In most cases he would know and address his staff by their Christian names.

If the management approach at Bathgate had been confrontational, at Gainsborough it could best be described as humane and co-operational. Unlike Bathgate, there were no unions and on the face of things there appeared to be no need for them. The boring and repetitive aspects of work in most factories involved in manufacturing and assembling on production lines was in the main not a factor on the shop floor of the Marshall factory.

Each tractor was built and assembled by a team of men who were responsible for the assembly of every part that went into it. They moved along the line with it, their names were on the build card alongside the model and chassis number, and they saw the completed tractor off the end of the line until it became the responsibility of the personnel in final inspection.

The thinking behind this was simple: it gave the men involved in the assembly process greater responsibility for getting it right first time, resulting in an end product of higher quality.

In those early months of 1982 one priority was to ensure a seamless supply of service parts to our distributors and dealers all over the world. It was estimated at that time that there were in excess of half a million Nuffield and Leyland tractors in service in the UK and in the many export markets that had become customers for our products since the launch of the first Nuffield tractor in 1948. Up until the purchase of the business by Marshall, all the parts for Nuffield and Leyland tractors came from British Leyland's computerised and largely automated parts centre at Cowley in Oxfordshire. Following Marshall's purchase of the Leyland tractor business, the parts were transferred to Gainsborough.

Ensuring an unbroken and efficient supply of parts to our customers was vitally important if we were to retain their confidence and business. Not only that, the highly profitable parts division brought in much needed cash for Marshall's fledgling wheeled tractor division.

While all this was going on, the train loads of finished tractors that had come down from Bathgate were receiving attention. Yes, they would eventually be sold with the Marshall name on the bonnet, but not before they had undergone the same rigorous quality checks and levels of inspection as those specified for Gainsborough-built tractors that would, later in the year, start rolling down the new production line. They were stripped down to a level where every major component could be inspected, checked and where necessary brought up to the Marshall standard of specification, build and finish.

One of the banners included in early advertising read 'Made Better by Marshall'. Surprisingly, some of our Scottish distributors took exception to this, saying that it was an implied criticism of the previous Bathgate-built tractors. These same Scottish distributors probably felt even more aggrieved later in 1982 when another series of Marshall advertising carried the headline 'A better British tractor will soon be here'. There is little doubt that the loss of a Scottish-built tractor to the Scottish dealer network made the Marshall product harder to sell north of the Border. The 'Made Better by Marshall' slogan, which was partly responsible for this, was certainly not well received in Scotland.

Although I have no record of the date when the first genuine Gainsborough-built tractor came off the production line, it was certainly before the end of 1982, possibly around October time. That was less than 10 months after the receipt of the first shipments of machine tools and componentry from Bathgate and other British Leyland plants. A remarkable achievement, the magnitude of which can only really be appreciated if you had been there to witness the levels of planning and work that went in to it.

Certainly, Gainsborough-built Marshall tractors based on the Leyland Harvest Gold design were on display at the Royal Smithfield Show of 1982.

I know I can speak for the likes of Kier Wyatt, Ray Runciman, Julian Bown, Alan Hawes, Ron Kettle and all other members of the team that less than a year earlier had been working for various sections of the Leyland tractor operation when I say that we felt a great sense of pride to be present at that particular Smithfield Show. The Marshall tractors on display there may have looked very similar to those of 12 months earlier, but few of us would have thought it possible to get a new production line up and running within such a short time scale.

It must be on record somewhere, but I have not been able to ascertain just when it was that members of the Marshall family ceased to have control of the huge business that continued to be known just everywhere by their world-famous name.

By 1982, when Leyland's tractor team moved to Gainsborough and joined forces with the existing Track Marshall organisation, the company operated under the chairmanship of Charles Nickerson. One of the characters that we came to know in our very early days at Gainsborough was an elderly gentleman called Henry Marshall. Henry, it transpired, was the last surviving member of the original family with a link to the company.

As so often happens when control of a business passes out of the hands of the founding family, its members are politely told that their services are no longer required, and so it was with Henry. It wasn't until Charles Nickerson acquired control of Track Marshall that Henry was invited to rejoin the company. When we first met him he was responsible for delivering mail round the various departments and for locating examples of past Marshall products from all over the world. They would eventually find their way into the museum that was planned in part of the refurbished factory complex.

Henry was very much a character and one of the old school. He had spent time working abroad for the family business, notably in India, where I believe a company still operates under the Marshall banner although, of course, under total Indian ownership. To say that Henry was delighted to be back working within the factory would be an understatement, and he would say, "If the Boss ever sacks me I shall still come to work!"

Henry owned a traction engine that carried his surname and he was rarely happier than when this was in steam and he was covered in grease, coal dust and soot. Henry passed away several years ago, but he was one of those people you feel proud and privileged to have been associated with.

As 1982 progressed, Marshall's tractor division continued to take shape. The transformation from what was very definitely a sow's ear when we first saw it in the February of that year quickly began to turn into something approaching a silk purse.

The general sales office arose from the rubble left by its previous owners into working accommodation every bit as good as anything we had been used to within the Leyland organisation. Keir Wyatt oversaw the entire sales, service and marketing operation, while David Ebrey and Dominic McClafferty managed technical service and warranty aspects of the new business.

BELOW LEFT:
One of the high-spec Explorer cabs made by Sekura is lowered onto a two-wheel drive tractor skid unit on the main tractor assembly line at the Britannia Works in 1983.

BELOW RIGHT:
With up to 500,000 Nuffield and Leyland tractors in the field, the importance of establishing an efficient spare parts operation was paramount to Marshall.

Peter Blair and locally recruited Cliff Haw controlled production programming and tractor dispatches. Ron Kettle and John Cubbin maintained contact with companies all over the world, who for so many years had been importing Leyland tractors, and in many cases the Nuffield range before that.

Just one little thought here about how methods of communication have changed. Each of the above individuals' desks would of course have had a telephone. Incredibly, though, there was only one fax machine in the entire factory and that was in the chairman's office, and none of us really knew what its capabilities were. E-mail was unheard of (surprise, surprise), as was the word processor, and typewriters were still just typewriters. Much of Ron Kettle's overseas communication would have been by telex.

TOP:
We really wondered what we'd let ourselves in for when we saw the area of the Britannia Works that was designated to become our general sales office!

RIGHT:
What a contrast to our first sight of the sales office area! After a lot of hard work, our new office was up and running and looking very smart by the end of 1982.

Although production of Gainsborough-built tractors hadn't started by the time the major summer shows of 1982 came along, it was decided that the new Marshall company should have a significant presence at both the Royal Highland Show in June and at the Royal Show two weeks later. Accordingly, under the slogan '134 Years of Commitment', a selection of the Bathgate-built 'Made Better by Marshall' tractors that had journeyed down to Gainsborough by train were exhibited at both events.

The '134 years' referred to the period between 1848, when the Marshall company started trading, and 1982 the year the Gainsborough firm took on the British Leyland tractor division and with it the support of thousands of customers who had been with the brand since the launch of the Nuffield Universal tractor in 1948.

There was understandably much concern about parts availability, service back-up and warranty coverage on recently purchased Bathgate-built tractors. The fact that the company was prepared to face owners, operators and the general farming public at both these major events was a demonstration of its serious intentions for the future.

Alan Hawes, Ray Runciman, Neil Spalding and I, together with our counterparts from the service and parts departments, manned the stands at both events. It was an interesting experience and different in many ways from the normal sell, sell, sell message that was usually the case at major shows.

A more subtle approach was the order of the day; we were after all laying a foundation for the future and building confidence within our existing customer base. We were also letting them see that what had been the Leyland tractor and what was soon to become the Marshall was in safe hands and would continue to be a product they could still buy with confidence.

While we had a number of the inevitable awkward customers and those who swore they would never buy another Leyland (particularly so, and perhaps not surprisingly, at the Highland Show), there was by and large a tremendous amount of goodwill and good wishes for the future success of the company. Even the good gentlemen of the press, who in my experience had never been disposed to write anything positive about the achievements of Leyland, seemed to display a more interested and supportive attitude.

Of critical importance was the attitude of the distributors and dealers, and almost without exception their response was totally positive.

Following hard on these first two public outings, the management of Marshall decided it was time to invite all the UK dealers to a meeting in order that company policy could be explained formally. This inaugural conference was held over two days in mid-September at Weston Park in Shropshire, the prestigious home of the Earl of Bradford.

Product-wise, a brief mention was made of the fact that development work had already started on tractors with more power than the 802 and 804 (82hp) models, which had been acquired as part of the purchase of the business from Leyland. Numerous tractors were on display and for the first time they were shown with the Marshall name on the bonnet and with other cosmetic changes that were to be introduced on Gainsborough-built tractors.

It was about this time (autumn 1982) that the fixing of machine tools, the laying down of production lines and most other aspects of tractor manufacture were complete and ready for work. One of the last items that had come down from Bathgate, the rolling road, was located at the end of the production line and formed part of the final inspection area.

For some reason the rolling road was never used to its full potential at Bathgate but not so at Gainsborough, where every tractor we built had to be put through its paces on the rolling road. It was designed to enable all aspects of the drive train to be tested under load so that every tractor coming off the line could be tested for gear, brake and PTO efficiency.

One of Marshall's adverts in 1982 read as follows: 'Marshall has been craft-building farm equipment since 1848. It made its first tractor in 1908. Marshall has never aspired to be an international giant. But it has grown, thanks to the impressive quality, reliability and technical innovation of its products. Now, the traditional pride and commitment of this 100 per cent British company are to be applied to the Leyland tractor range'.

The rolling road testing and its application to every single tractor produced in the Britannia Works was certainly an indication of the attention to detail and care that permeated through the division.

Marshall, the new owner of the former tractor division of British Leyland, might have been small by international standards, but as 1982 progressed its diminutive stature appeared not to matter a jot to all those who were working like demons to get the new venture off the ground.

Everything in virtually every aspect of the development of the product range and of the business generally was carried out to at least the same high standards, if not higher, than had previously been the case during the British Leyland era.

Take, for example, the first of two new Marshall sales brochures designed to promote the firm's range of cabbed tractors in the UK and most other European markets. Both were quality publications from front to back, featuring some really excellent photographs, mainly taken on our chairman's arable farm near Binbrook in the rolling Lincolnshire Wolds.

The brochure contained no mention of the recent Leyland parentage of the models it was promoting and instead harked back to an earlier generation. Under the headline 'Marshall Tractors…The Heritage', the new brochure proudly associated the new Gainsborough-built tractors with what was considered by many to be the Rolls Royce of tractors, the Nuffield, and with an earlier world-famous Gainsborough model, the single-cylinder Field Marshall.

The first page included an archive picture of a well-cared-for Nuffield 4/60, complete with its BMC Diesel badge on the front grille, sold originally I think by one of the very early Nuffield distributors, Sycamores of Ramsey in Huntingdonshire. It was accompanied by a smaller inset picture of a single-cylinder Field Marshall Series III.

On the facing page, under the headline 'Marshall Tractors…The Future', was a superbly staged view of a Gainsborough-built 802 and 604 in a sunny harvest field setting. The association between the old and new was clear. Remember, this was back in 1982 when the reputation of the Nuffield tractor marque was somewhat fresher in the minds of many farmers than it is today. The message was very clear and very effective.

The design and pictorial impact of this marvellous brochure is still impressive even today. It has to be a must for the serious collector of tractor memorabilia and I have it on good authority that mint examples now have a price tag of at least £10.

The brochure's strength as a sales aid was illustrated by the fact that its well-written narrative was translated into several European languages, including French, Italian, Swedish and Danish. Gainsborough-built tractors were exported to these countries, among others, within the so-called Common Market and further afield, but more of this later.

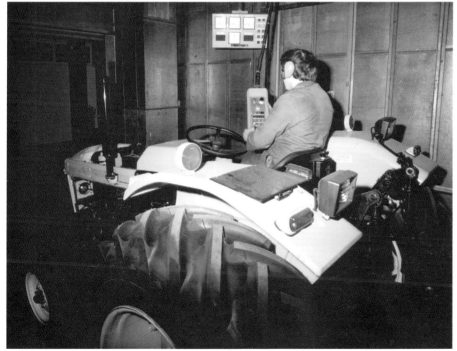

TOP:
The 1982 Royal Show came too early for Marshall to exhibit its own Gainsborough-built tractors, but it still managed to put on an impressive display using the buffer stock inherited from Leyland.

LEFT:
Each tractor had its transmission, brakes and power take-off tested and recorded on a rolling road. This Marshall 702 platform tractor was destined for export.

The same format was used again for a second time when it was decided that literature of a similar quality was needed to help promote the sales of cabless tractors in markets where a more basic specification was the order of the day. In the main this was outside Europe, although a number of cabless tractors did go to Portugal and in much smaller quantities to Italy.

By the time the second brochure was in the pipeline, sometime in 1983, I had joined Ron Kettle in export sales and so we both had a vested interest in ensuring the relevance of the story-line around which it was built, together with the accuracy of its pictorial content.

TOP:
Marshall's stand at the 1982 Smithfield Show was an impressive affair. It marked the end of an incredible year of achievement for the company.

RIGHT:
Explaining what Marshall had to offer on the stand of Marshall's French importer at the 1983 SIMA Show in Paris. Peter Wheelton, our publicity manager, is second from right.

Producing publicity material wasn't an entirely new task to us: we had worked together on several of the first Leyland brochures when we were based up in Bathgate. On an earlier occasion we had been asked to check over text produced by a copywriter working with the Edinburgh-based design agency employed to produce an important new brochure. What Ron and I read on that occasion was so far removed from the realities of tractor work and farming practices that the changes we made resulted in a complete rewrite. The agency copywriter was far from pleased and declined to work with us again; it was, however, our version that eventually appeared in print.

The difference with the new Marshall brochure was that we were able to start with a clean sheet of paper. It is certainly always easier to put your own thoughts and ideas into words rather than trying to put right somebody else's work. It was, however, a major project and one that could not be done effectively during the day-to-day comings and goings of the busy sales office in Gainsborough. Ron and I ended up burning many hours of near midnight oil on the project. The compensation, if any was needed, was being able to be out in the field during what proved to be, in the main, the long, hot summer of 1983.

We were working with a photographic agency to ensure the accuracy of the pictorial content of the new brochure. In this respect it was thought unnecessary to go to the expense of taking tractors overseas. As a result, all the export photographs were in fact taken in carefully chosen locations in north Lincolnshire.

I suppose it might be said that Ron and I were nothing if not versatile. I believe it stemmed from our farming background, our agricultural college training and the 20 or so years we spent working with the British Motor Corporation and British Leyland, and a product that had become very much a part of our lives. Not that it was just Ron and I who could be classed as versatile. Virtually every member of the ex-Leyland team now working in Gainsborough was capable of wearing several different caps and did so willingly on many occasions.

My move to join Ron Kettle on export sales was brought about when the previous incumbent, John Cubbin, sadly died following a short illness. John had done substantial business for Leyland in most central and South American countries and was a much respected member of the team. The resulting change meant that Scotland and northern England needed a new area manager, and so it was that Ian Jack accepted an invitation to rejoin the team.

Since the transfer of production from Bathgate Ian had been responsible for sales at the Carlisle branch of Oliver & Snowdon, which by this time had become a John Deere dealer. He gained valuable experience on the retail side of the business and, without doubt, Ian's work with Marshall in what had been my area of responsibility was all the more effective as a result.

At about the same time, another colleague, whom I first met during my first two months at the original Nuffield factory at Ward End, Birmingham in 1962, and who was not originally asked to come to Gainsborough in the first instance, also received an invitation to join the Marshall team. Martin Stokes was more than happy to renew his association with the product range he knew inside out, both technically and operationally.

It seemed to be the case that there was no problem in employing the right people in the right numbers. It was encouraging to see men such as Ian and Martin becoming part of the team again. As the manufacturing facilities became established inside Britannia Works, and tractor production started to roll, personnel of their experience and commitment would be essential to help compete with the growing number of imported tractors appearing on the UK market during the early 1980s.

Prior to my involvement in export sales I had been to Italy to assist in the launch of the Synchro range; to Morocco with Ron Kettle, where we conducted a series of product introductions to dealers following shipment of the first part of an order for 500 Leyland 272s; plus several visits to Mahon & McPhillips, the long-standing importer in Eire.

Of course, the export of the earlier Nuffield tractors originally began shortly after the first Ward End tractors came off the production line in 1948. Except for what were then communist bloc countries, there is hardly a country in the world where Nuffield and Leyland tractors had not been exported.

Here is an interesting statistic. Today there are still over 6200 Leylands registered for use on the roads of Finland, plus possibly hundreds more unregistered tractors at work on farms in that country, and this is 30 years after the last Leyland tractor was produced. It so happens that Finland was the largest export market for Leyland tractors during the Bathgate era. The importer, Kesko OY, with headquarters in Helsinki, was fairly typical of importers in most other countries. The company operated departments for wholesale and retail sales, marketing and sales promotion, parts and technical service, and demonstrations.

In the case of Kesko, the whole operation was headed up by a general manager called Antii Jusila, a man full of enthusiasm for the tractor range, something that was very much in evidence right across the staffing structure of the company.

When I worked on export sales during the Marshall era, much of my time was devoted to Scandinavia, especially Sweden and Denmark. In Sweden the importer was a privately owned business known as Brorssons, based in the small town of Mariennelund in the south of the country. Many of Sweden's farmers have a decent acreage of forestry and it was important that tractors should be sufficiently versatile to enable them to work for part of the year at least in the different conditions required in the timber industry.

Led by Arni Ivarsson, general manager of the tractor division, together with the forestry department of a leading Swedish university, modifications were made to the Explorer cabbed four-wheel drive Leyland and Marshall 704 and 804 models. The aim was to make them more attractive to timber growers whose agricultural tractors didn't normally offer fully reversible seats and other refinements necessary to achieve maximum output when working in the forest. Brorssons exhibited at all the major forestry exhibitions and the Leyland and Marshall Skogstraktor or Forestry Tractor was responsible for a large proportion of the many tractors we sold in Sweden.

Agriculture in Denmark isn't dissimilar to that found in many parts of the UK and the importer, DOMI (Dansk Oversoisk Motor Industri), based in Copenhagen, was the largest privately owned company in the country. It began an association with

Morris Motors when Lord Nuffield was involved in the day-to-day running of the company that bore his family name. Through DOMI, Denmark became a major market for Morris cars, commercial vehicles and, of course, Nuffield, Leyland and Marshall tractors.

Again, DOMI had its own separate agricultural division, which for many years was headed up by general manager Mogens Molberg. On his retirement in the late 1970s he was replaced by his sales manager, Aage Moller. Aage, together with his service manager Kaj Kroger and a highly competent parts operation, was responsible for the sale of many hundreds of Leyland and Marshall tractors into Denmark.

During the Gainsborough era, DOMI saw a potential for the sale of the Track Marshall 135 crawler. A demonstration unit, complete with Dowdeswell plough, was shipped over and a programme of well-organised public demonstrations put in hand. Sadly, however, the untimely demise of Marshall in 1985 meant that this couldn't be capitalised on in terms of sales, but DOMI did become the national importer for Dowdeswell.

Across Europe, Nuffield and Leyland tractors sold into Holland, Belgium, France, Spain, Portugal and Austria. Italy began taking large quantities of Nuffields through its Turin-based importer, Vittorio Cantatore. This company developed its own four-wheel drive version of the Nuffield Universal and examples of these can still be found at work on Italian farms.

My involvement with sales into the Italian market began in the early part of the Marshall era, when a family-owned business known as Agritractor became the importer. This company had been a Nuffield and Leyland regional dealer since the early Cantatore days and had retailed over 1000 Nuffield tractors in that time. Its enthusiasm

A Marshall 804 Skogstraktor or Forestry Tractor in action at a forestry equipment demonstration in Sweden in the mid-1980s.

149

for the tractor was well illustrated by a fully refurbished Universal Four that at one time (and possibly still does) took pride of place in its large showroom. The tractor, serial number 787-3034, was produced at Ward End in September 1957 and was sold by the company in the same year to a farmer in the nearby town of Savigliano.

I was told by the late and much respected Tomaso Racca, who started the company and was personally responsible for most of those 1000 Nuffield sales, that today there are still in excess of 5000 Nuffield, Leyland and Marshall tractors working on Italian farms.

Apart from Morocco, my export travels never took me outside Europe and Scandinavia. However, colleagues such as Jim Taylor, Ron Kettle, John Cubbin, Peter Hitchings and Neil Spalding, to name but a few, regularly travelled right across the world in pursuit of business. They kept the production lines running and provided continuing employment for our employees, not to mention a useful source of income for the company.

The various markets are too numerous to list here, but the USA and Canada were major countries, as were South Africa, Australia and New Zealand. Nuffield and Leyland tractors were sold into most African countries that formed part of what was the British Empire, most countries in South America, Malaysia, the Philippines, Thailand, Greece and Turkey.

In a small way Marshall was also now an importer; the 302, built by BMC Sinai at their Izmir factory in Turkey, was being brought in to Gainsborough in crated CKD form.

Rated at 30hp, the 302 was born out of the original BMC Mini tractor and the later Nuffield 4/25 and Leyland 154. Its introduction at the lower end of the Marshall range was designed to provide a lightweight agricultural tractor, one that would be appropriate to the work of councils, sports grounds and light industrial users.

An area within the factory had been reserved for assembly of the crated components and for fitment of the Veroc quiet cab. This was yet another part of the new Marshall tractor division that was up and running by very early 1983.

THE 1983 MARSHALL RANGE

MODEL	POWER	RETAIL PRICE
302 Q cab	30hp	£6,023
302 cabless	30hp	£5,148
502 QM cab	44.5hp	£8,039
602 QM cab	60hp	£9,269
602 Explorer cab	60hp	£9,866
604 QM cab	60hp	£11,660
604 Explorer cab	60hp	£12,257
702 QM cab	71hp	£9,960
702 Explorer cab	71hp	£10,557
704 QM cab	71hp	£12,762
802 Explorer cab	82hp	£11,410
804 Explorer cab	82hp	£14,188

Ten

Ask and Thou Shall be Given

Way back in the early to mid-1980s the average size of tractor sold in the UK was in the region of 80hp. While modest by today's standards, this figure still represented a major increase on the average size of 20 or so years earlier, when tractors such as the 60hp Nuffield 4/60, one of the models I cut my teeth on, were regarded as big machines.

Although I don't have any statistical records to refer to, so I may be a little wide of the mark, I believe the average power of the 40,000 or so new tractors sold each year in the UK during the mid-1960s stood at a miserly 45hp. Moreover, it was almost possible to count on the fingers of two hands how many of those were four-wheel drive.

It so happened that the largest tractors in the range that Marshall of Gainsborough acquired with the purchase of the British Leyland tractor division in 1982 were, at 82hp, just about of average size for the time. The models concerned were the 802 (2WD) and the 804 (4WD), both far and away the biggest selling models in the Leyland range. They became so once again when tractors began to roll off the new production line at Gainsborough at the end of 1982.

The directors of the company would have been very well aware, however, that the market trend towards ever more horsepower was firmly established and moving on at an increasing pace. A flagship with 82hp might be all well and good in the short term, but it would not provide a sufficiently broad base on which to build a secure future for a tractor manufacturing facility. Not even for one of the moderate proportions that had been planned for the small market town of Gainsborough in north Lincolnshire.

I have already mentioned the product planning responsibilities I was given during the time I worked at Bathgate, as well as in the sales and marketing headquarters of British Leyland's tractor division at Preston in Lancs.

Within that huge conglomerate there were some very strict product development procedures, based on what was known as a Product Investigation Letter, or PIL for short. There were no short cuts and the PIL procedures had to be followed to the letter before any design engineer or draughtsman could even put pencil to paper to start work on a modification to an existing design, or to initiate something completely new.

Marshall demonstration driver Richmond Leeson shows off the 904XL's ploughing abilities at the dealer launch at Binbrook in Lincolnshire in 1984.

CENTRE:
Marshall sales director Kier Wyatt explains the features of the company's new 904XL and 100 Series models during the dealer launch in Lincolnshire.

RIGHT:
The introduction of the 92hp Marshall 904XL in 1984 was welcome news for the company's dealer network.

By and large the procedures were sound and worked effectively, and I came to know their complexities pretty well.

Here in Gainsborough, I was a member of the sales team and, quite rightly, had no involvement in plans for what shape the Marshall product range might take in the future. To this day I do not know what form the product planning procedures took, who chaired product planning meetings or who sanctioned the necessary capital expenditure.

In the Bathgate days such meetings were almost invariably chaired by the engineering director, the often difficult, outspoken, tough, abrasive but fair and very knowledgeable, Bob Beresford. Perhaps in a privately run company there was much more informality but, as I say, I don't know.

However, in whatever way decisions were made in Britannia Works they were certainly made quickly. Indeed, it was not long before news filtered through concerning work on a project designed to overcome just about the only shortcoming of the Bathgate-designed Synchro gearbox – the lack of a true creep-speed gear facility.

The Gainsborough development work involved the design of a sandwich box that could be fitted between the clutch housing and the front face of the Synchro box itself. Once in production it was made available on all four-cylinder models, both two- and four-wheel drive, and provided a further six forward and two reverse ratios, resulting in a total of 15 forward and 5 reverse gears. It also lengthened the wheelbase by approximately 8in and gave rise to the new model designation of XL, this standing for Extra Length.

The XL versions of the 802 and 804 quickly became popular and today, 20 years later, they are well known and sought after on the second-hand market. What is not as well known is that there was, under development, a second version of the new transmission, designed to provide completely clutchless changes between gears. I had the opportunity of driving it on one or two occasions. I hesitate to call it a Multi-Power type of arrangement because almost certainly it would have been superior to any of its counterparts of that type in the early 1980s. Sadly, for reasons I will touch upon later, this transmission never saw the light of day in production.

Following hard on the heels of the introduction of the XL models came the first indication that the company really was aware of the need to get into horsepower categories higher than those it had inherited from Leyland.

Earlier in my story I might have erroneously given the impression that the closure of Bathgate's tractor production line in C block led to the whole factory being closed down. In fact, commercial vehicle and engine production continued after the tractor division moved out.

Importantly, the plant's superb series of long-stroke Leyland 4/98 diesel engines continued to be available for the Gainsborough-built tractors. At the request of and in conjunction with Marshall's engineering department, a new version using a slightly higher level of turbo-charging and a Simms Minimec in-line injection pump was produced to provide 92hp at 2200rpm.

I know that I am very much out of touch these days with the intricacies of diesel engine design but, given the choice, and based on more than a few years of experience,

I would still opt for a good, low-revving, economical, long-lasting and relatively quiet diesel engine, with the emphasis very definitely on a long piston stroke. In my book, long stroke and high torque well down the rev range go hand in hand.

For what it is worth, the new 92hp Leyland engine, as fitted to what became known as the Marshall 904XL, weighed in with 238lb/ft of torque at only 1600rpm.

The 904XL specification was just about right in areas other than just pure horse-power and torque. The standard specification included twin assister rams to provide a linkage lift capacity of 2906kg, a 12in transmission clutch, new Carraro front axle with limited-slip differential and a completely new 27-gallon fuel tank.

Product planning systems and procedures or not, the requirements of the market place were being met very accurately by the new Marshall organisation.

Gainsborough, of course, is close to some of the largest areas of arable farming in the UK. In my view, product development at Bathgate suffered partly from the fact that there was absolutely no truly heavy arable land for miles around. Step out of the factory gate at Gainsborough and you were virtually surrounded by it, on either side of the river Trent. Then, of course, there was the company chairman, Charles Nickerson, who was an arable farmer on a considerable scale.

To say that engineering manager Mike Barnes, who had been working in a similar position at Bathgate, and his new Gainsborough-based team were coming up with the goods in remarkably short time would be an understatement. But then this same sentiment applied to so much that was being achieved in the still early days of that still young company. What else might already be on the drawing board and see the light of day in the coming months and years?

The indications were that 92hp would not be the limit of the company's aspirations and ambitions. Of course, up in Bathgate the six-cylinder version of the excellent 98-series of Leyland tractor engines was still coming off the production line.

DOMI, our Danish importer, arranged for this group of dealers to visit the factory in 1984. While there, they were able to see this consignment of tractors leave the plant for their home country.

THE MARSHALL 904XL

Engine	Leyland 4/98TT
Cylinders	4 turbo
Capacity	3.77 litres (230cu.in)
Max power	92hp
Clutch	12in dry plate
Gearbox	15F/5R
PTO	540/1000
Linkage	Category II
Lift capacity	2906kg

I know that on occasion during my meanderings through my career story I leave myself wide open to the accusation of bias. I am aware of this when I extol the virtues of most of the products with which I was associated during the 30 or so years I worked for the British Motor Corporation, British Leyland and the Marshall companies at Gainsborough and Scunthorpe.

Of course, being patriotic and loyal to the core, I make absolutely no apologies for this! By and large the products were very good and competitive in the tractor market place. As a result of the considerable volumes that were exported over the years, they also made a significant contribution to the commercial strength of this nation of ours. Sadly, this is a claim that can't be made by the present-day UK tractor manufacturing industry.

So, here I go again! In the 21 years since I have ceased to be directly involved in the tractor business, nothing I have seen or read anywhere has yet to convince me that there has been a finer tractor engine than that known as the Leyland 6/98, produced at British Leyland's Bathgate factory in Scotland.

By the way, for those who have never had the opportunity of working with Leyland engines, the first digit in the type designation refers to the number of cylinders and the second to the bore of those cylinders. The 6/98 has, therefore, six cylinders with a bore of 98mm; both the four- and six-cylinder versions had a stroke of 125mm. In both cases this resulted in a long-stroke configuration and, for the 6/98 engine, a swept volume of 5.65 litres. I'm adamant it was one of the finest tractor engines anywhere in that particular horsepower category.

So why am I writing at such length about this great tractor engine, when the last time it had been used in an agricultural application was in the not-very-successful Leyland 285, 485, 2100 and 4100 models? At that time there were two versions – the 85hp 6/98DT (Derated Tractor) and the 100hp 6/98NT (Normal Tractor).

Fairly early in the life of the new Marshall tractor company a small quantity of 6/98NT engines appeared in the Goods Inward area and were quickly despatched

BELOW LEFT:
Marshall's 100-4 was comfortable with five furrows. This publicity picture, with field test driver John Cook at the wheel, was used on the front cover of Marshall's 100 Series sales brochure.

BELOW RIGHT:
Marshall sales director Keir Wyatt with the first Marshall 100-4 tractor to leave the line at the Britannia Works, Gainsborough, probably in October 1984.

behind the closed doors of the engineering department. Around the same time some of us in tractor sales were told that somebody was being quoted as having said: 'What we (i.e. the company) wanted was a Fendt-type tractor at a Ford-type price.'

I never heard this being said, nor did I ever find out who was supposed to have said it. On the basis that such a recipe was, in all probability, unachievable, it's unlikely to have been said in quite that way anyway.

Nevertheless, when coupled with the arrival from Bathgate of the six-cylinder engines, it did lead us to the conclusion that work must be under way to engineer tractors capable of making use of the horsepower and performance characteristics of the Leyland 6/98 power unit.

In the certain knowledge that there was no point in doing what Leyland had earlier attempted during the 1970s – mating the 6/98 to a mid-range transmission – it seemed this new development programme would be a long-term one. After all, designing a new 100hp-type gearbox would, with the best will in the world, be a long, involved and expensive exercise.

TOP:
Marshall had performed miracles in bringing their new 100 Series to the market in such a short space of time, and these men, part of the assembly team, played a big role.

RIGHT:
Although we claimed this was the first Marshall 100-4 to leave the Britannia Works, it was actually a set-up picture aimed at breeding confidence in the brand.

Having said all this, I remember taking a small party of dealers from Ireland around the factory during the late summer of 1983. Factory tours always included visits to the Track Marshall production area and to the tractor parts stores, both of which were in the same section as the engineering department for the wheeled tractor division.

Some of the visitors, as often happens on such occasions, had wandered on ahead of the main party and could be seen in the distance, outside the engineering department, standing around what appeared to be nothing more than a skid unit on wheels, painted in the old Leyland blue.

It was coming under close scrutiny from a curious and knowledgeable gentleman from Ireland. By the time the rest of the group, including myself, caught up they had recognised the engine as one they all knew well, a six-cylinder Leyland 6/98, and could see that the front axle and gearbox were from ZF, the German drivetrain specialist. The Leyland engine was mounted in massive cast chassis members and the rear three-point linkage, which looked huge in proportion, bore some resemblance to that of the Track Marshall 135 crawler and appeared to benefit from two large external assister rams.

TOP:
The Marshall 100 Series dealer launch took place at Binbrook, Lincs, in October 1984 on land belonging to company chairman Charles Nickerson.

LEFT:
Deliveries of the Marshall 100-4 didn't begin until February 1985, so the unit used at the dealer launch in late 1984, registration number B148 BFW, was probably the second or third off the line.

Was this, then, the first public viewing of the Fendt-type tractor that had been talked about around the works? Whatever it was, there was no doubt that this early prototype was the basis for what, in just over 12 months' time, would become the new Marshall 100 Series, a range that consisted of the two-wheel drive 100-2 and four-wheel drive 100-4 models, both of 100hp, as well as the four-wheel drive 115 4 of 115hp.

The new models were officially unveiled to the public at the Royal Smithfield Show at Earls Court in London in December 1984. I well remember our stand being as busy if not busier that year than it had been in all the 20 or so years I had been attending the show with Nuffield and Leyland.

The two new models featured prominently within the high quality Marshall display and on their own would have been sufficient to ensure a hectic week for the sales team, which included experienced professionals such as Martin Stokes, Ian Jack, Andy McMeechan, Neil Spalding and the ever enthusiastic Alan Hawes.

BELOW LEFT:
The press launch for the new 100 Series tractors was held in Marshall's superb new museum area at the Britannia Works in Gainsborough.

BELOW RIGHT:
Exhibits displayed in Marshall's impressive new museum included the prototype Standard tractor, sectional Nuffield and Marshall single-cylinder tractors, plus Henry Marshall's steam engine.

However, to ensure that the Marshall stand was the undoubted star of that particular Royal Smithfield Show, we decided to exhibit an example of one of the company's earlier products alongside the two latest models. This took the form of a 1908 Marshall Colonial oil-engined tractor weighing 15 tons! The Colonial had originally been exported to Australia but had been brought back to the UK, fully restored into running condition, and then placed on display in the company museum in Gainsborough.

Initially the management of Earls Court were not prepared to allow this monster into the show because of its colossal weight. This was hardly surprising as our stand was on a removable display floor above the area that was normally flooded for the Boat Show! The organisers were adamant that the floor would not be strong enough to support the weight of the giant Colonial.

A lesser firm might have bowed to their opposition, but not the young and aggressive Marshall company, which was almost as proud of its heritage as it was of the two new models it had just produced. In the end special supports were put in place directly below where the Colonial was to stand.

By today's standards, the specification of the new Marshall 100 Series was not excessively complicated. However, the machines did come with several novel features: they were among the first to use the Bosch system of electronic bottom link sensing and, unusually, the entire hydraulic system, with a massive 10,000lb lift capacity, was completely external.

The ZF transmission used in the 100 Series provided 20 forward and nine reverse ratios, with synchromesh for the range and gear selection.

The transmission might have come from ZF of Germany, but the method of selecting the gears was pure Marshall. The gear levers and the gate through which they were shifted worked via a simple forward and reverse shift, together with a twisting motion of the extra large gear knobs, in place of the normal shift across the gate.

This enabled the levers to be placed much closer together than usual and made maximum use of the available cab floor space.

There was a massive 40-gallon fuel tank, which formed part of the bonnet line, and the cab was a high-spec version of the well-accepted Sekura Explorer unit already fitted to the mid-range four-cylinder models. The auto-hitch was probably the first to extend rearwards as it lowered towards the ring hitch of the trailer, thereby providing much improved visibility for the driver.

All in all, I remember that the new Marshall 100 Series tractors created considerable interest in the market place.

They also did no end of good for the credibility of the company, not least because they showed that we had the expertise and resources to bring new models to the market in a relatively short space of time.

Granted, it did take a bit longer than we would have liked to get these brand new models into production, but the demand was there and farmers in the mid-1980s seemed prepared to wait for them, irrespective of whether the rumoured Fendt/Ford combination of specification and price applied or not.

THE MARSHALL 100 SERIES

	100-2	100-4	115-4
Engine	Leyland 6/98NT	Leyland 6/98NT	Leyland 6/98NT
Cylinders	6	6	6 turbo
Max power	103.5hp	103.5hp	115hp
Clutch		13in single plate	
Transmission		20 forward/nine reverse	
Linkage		Category 2 quick connect	
Lift capacity		4540kg (10,000lb)	
Length		4.17m	
Weight	4670kg	4915kg	4915kg
Turning radius	5.25m	5.77m	5.77m
Fuel tank		182 litres	

The introduction of the Marshall 100-2 and 100-4 tractors at the Royal Smithfield Show in 1984 was very definitely a milestone for the Gainsborough-based company. The 100 Series launch was also something of a milestone for the rest of the UK tractor industry, not least because during the late 1970s and early 1980s there had been a period of stagnation in the development of completely fresh designs and new technology.

Most of the major manufacturers appeared to be taking stock of their positions in the market place. Any such product development, if that is what it could be called, revolved around little more than modifications and updates to well-tried models that in many cases had been around for quite a considerable time. I seem to recall that much the same could also be said for most of the continental tractor manufacturers.

I say the Marshall 100 Series were milestones because they were just about the only completely new models to be introduced by any manufacturer for a number of years. In many ways the 100 Series tractors, and the company that developed them, could be said to be taking the lead and bucking the trend.

Not that Marshalls had any thoughts of trying to compete with the majors in terms of sales and market share, at least not just yet. The company knew its place and its position in the tractor business. In spite of all that had been achieved in the little over two years since its formation, it had, at this stage, no plans to be anything other than a smallish, completely British-owned and controlled manufacturer capable of producing around 3000 tractors per year.

The plan was that each of these tractors would be produced to the highest possible quality of build. From a design and specification point of view, the range would provide an acceptable level of sophistication, but would not exceed the requirements of the average farmer, as seems to be very much the case in these early years of the 21st century.

In terms of mass-production, 3000 tractors per annum were, of course, very much at the bottom end of the manufacturing graph. British Leyland's tractor factory at Bathgate,

One of Marshall's oldest tractors, a Colonial of 1908, was displayed alongside the new 100 Series models at the official launch at the 1984 Royal Smithfield Show.

on which Marshall production at Gainsborough was based, was capable of building between 25,000 and 30,000 units each year, though it rarely achieved this sort of output. However, even this was relatively small fry in the world-wide scale of things.

However, when the young Marshall company introduced the 100-2, 100-4 and 115-4 models at the 1984 Royal Smithfield Show, its tractor division was effectively only two years old. Everything it had done and continued to do was very close to being right as far as the requirements of the dealers and farmers across the UK and further afield were concerned.

Even the gentlemen of the agricultural press, a band usually distinctly difficult to please and get on-side, were virtually unanimous in singing the praises of everything they saw and heard in Gainsborough. One wrote about 'small being very beautiful' and another described the factory as a 'cathedral of excellence'. What greater praise could any company wish for, particularly when the new 904XL and the three new six-cylinder tractors were so well received into the bargain?

By the time the 100 Series tractors were ready to be launched, most of the rebuilding and refurbishing work on that 'cathedral of excellence' at Gainsborough was complete. Included within the works was a really first-class museum-cum-showroom facility. It was in the museum where the UK dealers and our friends from the agricultural and the national press were wined and dined and given the opportunity to inspect the Marshall 100-4. Conditions here were in contrast to the dealer launch on a wind-swept field on the chairman's farm in the middle of the Lincolnshire Wolds.

The museum was primarily established to house examples of Marshall products built during its long history. The curator was the late Henry Marshall, the last surviving member of the family. He was given the task by the chairman of finding products from around the world and bringing them back to their original place of manufacture, where they could be refurbished and placed in the museum.

This Marshall 100-4 with dual front wheels and Herbst half-tracks was one of two units supplied for peat harvesting in the south-west of Scotland.

Henry was present in the museum for the launch of the latest new products to carry his family name. Standing only a few yards from the 100-4 was his very own traction engine carrying the registration number E9624. Alongside this was a 1937 Marshall steam roller and a Marshall model M single-cylinder tractor of around the same vintage. Other exhibits were a sectioned Field Marshall Series I, a Nuffield Universal from around 1950 and one of the few remaining examples of the prototype Standard tractor which I have discussed earlier in this story.

At the opposite end of the museum, close to the imposing reception area through which all factory visitors had to pass, stood the massive 15-ton Colonial tractor which had given the organisers of the 1984 Royal Smithfield Show so much to worry about.

There was, however, no sign of a Leyland tractor, the immediate predecessor to the Marshall range of the early 1980s. It was considered, rightly or wrongly, that the Leyland marque was not compatible with the image that Marshall wished to project. As a result, the Leyland name was not included in the corporate family tree. Certainly Nuffield, which in its day was often referred to as the Rolls-Royce of tractors, was very acceptable, but Leyland was definitely not.

Orders for the 100-2 and 100-4 models were coming in nicely during the early months of 1985. Production worked hard to meet the demand and to reduce delivery times. Meanwhile, production of the established four-cylinder models was moving along at a reasonable rate, although for those of us in the sales department it was never fast enough.

That is not to say it was not a frustrating time for both myself and Ron Kettle. It was our job to generate export business and we were frequently frustrated by the priority that was given to the home market. In spite of this, some memorable successes were notched up with sales outside of these shores. Ron sold numerous less-cab platform tractors to the USA, Canada and several South American countries, as well as to South Africa and Zaire.

My own responsibilities were in Scandinavia, Europe and North Africa. Sweden and Denmark became particularly good markets for the Gainsborough-built range, which was also exported to Ireland, Holland, France and notably to Italy. The single largest export order came from Cogem in Tunisia and involved 50 platform Marshall 502s, this being the three-cylinder model powered by the Perkins A3.152 engine.

During the latter months of 1984 and into 1985 the factory was visited by numerous overseas importers, usually made up of senior directors, sales personnel and regional dealers. To many the Marshall name conveyed absolutely nothing. As famous as it was in some quarters, it was just not that familiar to many of our importers or their customers.

To arrive in the small town of Gainsborough and see the factory with its busy production line, the vast service and parts department for Nuffield and Leyland, and the new Marshall models, dispelled any doubts about the ambitions of this small, new tractor company. Also impressive was the Track Marshall crawler production line and a museum of which any company, large or small, could be justly proud.

The Marshall works was certainly a 'cathedral of excellence' in early 1985. So much had been achieved since 1982; what could possibly be expected during the remainder of the year and beyond?

Eleven

Saved and off
to Scunthorpe

Writing about my career highlights has always been a pleasure because up until the middle of 1985 everything was going so well. Targets were being met and exceeded, important new models were being introduced, and new companies were joining the dealer network at home and abroad. I was a member of a hard-working team whose level of dedication to the product range was probably the highest of any company anywhere in the world.

I am convinced this was the case during the 20 years I spent working with the Nuffield and Leyland tractor ranges, and again starting in early 1982 when many of Leyland's tractor team moved south to Marshall.

The period from February 1982, when the transfer of Leyland's tractor business from the Scottish factory at Bathgate to Marshall at Gainsborough began, through to the Royal Smithfield Show of 1984, was one of tremendous achievement and apparent success.

However, as we moved into 1985 it quickly became obvious that the worldwide tractor market wasn't what it had been and the demand had softened considerably. Generally the industry had considerable over capacity and, as a result, the levels of competitive pricing and discounting became even more cut-throat, especially by the major names.

Much larger companies than Marshall had already found or were finding the going very tough. By this time County Commercial Cars, Muir-Hill and Roadless Traction had fallen on hard times, and implement manufacturers Bamlett and Bamfords were also facing an uphill struggle, leading ultimately to their demise.

David Brown, which at one time had been wholly British owned, had by now become part of J. I. Case and was controlled from the USA. The giant International Harvester organisation had lost hundreds of millions, probably billions, of dollars between 1980 and 1983 and had to sell its agricultural division to J. I. Case in late 1984. International Harvester at nearby Doncaster had mothballed its Carr Hill factory, where final assembly of tractors took place, in 1983, and had transferred all assembly operations to Wheatley Hall Road. Then there was Massey Ferguson, another huge farm machinery company, which in 1980 had been on the brink of bankruptcy after a run of disastrous losses. Its workforce and manufacturing capacity had been dramatically slashed in the early 1980s and it strove to stay afloat.

There was even talk that the mighty Ford Motor Company was looking at ways of divesting itself of its tractor business. It did eventually succeed in hiving off its tractor and farm machinery division when it sold out to Fiat in 1991.

However, in Gainsborough, conditions appeared to be rather different. The Marshall Group, which back in 1982 consisted of Marshall Tractors and Track Marshall, continued to expand, not only by internal growth and development, but by further acquisitions.

By 1985 the factory complex also housed a company involved in the design and manufacture of specialist turf maintenance machinery, known as Nickerson Turf Master. This was followed by a very specialist operation which was developing a process to convert most forms of fibrous plant waste material into something comparable to chipboard or hardboard. It traded under the title of Compak Systems Limited and appeared to have virtually unlimited potential, selling the machinery and plant which produced the board to developing countries. In many ways, the Britannia Works appeared to be immune to all the problems in the tractor and farm machinery business.

That was until May 1985, when Marshall came out with the shock announcement that it was making 35 of its workforce redundant. This might not have seemed like a significant number to an outsider, but those of us still employed by the firm knew that the job losses represented around a 10% reduction of the total workforce, a not insignificant proportion.

Most of the job losses were in manufacturing and translated into a reduction in production levels of both crawlers and wheel tractors. For the very first time it was becoming apparent that all was not as it should be within Gainsborough's 'cathedral of excellence'. Later in the year short-time working was introduced as a further means of lowering production levels. As I remember, this was probably during July or August.

As I said earlier, it is comparatively easy to write about times and experiences when things are going well. So from here on in it gets much more difficult. I remember one afternoon in late September working at my desk at Britannia Works, getting to grips with some export sales business. If my memory serves me correctly, Ron Kettle had only recently returned to the office after supervising the loading of a batch of half a dozen or so cabless Marshall 702s into containers for dispatch that afternoon to one of his distributors in Equador.

Ron had seen the containers on to the lorries of Bradshaws, the efficient and obliging Gainsborough-based haulier who moved all our tractors out of the works, whether for the home market or export. Ron had left them at the factory gate as the drivers and our gate security man sorted out the last of the dispatch paperwork.

Sometime around 4pm on that day, I think it was 25 September, Rob Mackay, an assembly shop foreman and a no-nonsense Scotsman who had come down from Bathgate back in 1982, came in to the office. He stood before Ron, myself and Peter Blair, who was in charge of all dispatches and documentation, and said that a group of people had just arrived in the car park, closed the factory gates and would not allow the Equador tractors to leave.

Nobody in sales, marketing or service had been told to expect the arrival of these people who, on the face of it, had just appeared out of the blue. Within a few minutes they had secured the gates with a lock and chain, to which only they had the key. Britannia Works and all the companies it housed was in receivership and to those of us who worked there that is exactly how it happened.

The local Gainsborough paper, dated 2 October, carried the page three headline 'Body Blow at Marshalls'. It went on to state that 'The announcement that Gainsborough tractor firm, Marshalls, have called in receivers has sent shock waves through the town. Over 300 jobs could face the axe, although financial experts currently handling Marshall's affairs have said no redundancies are planned for the time being.'

TOP:
Marshall and Track Marshall faced an uncertain future when the company that owned them, Marshall Limited, went into receivership on 25 September 1985.

LEFT:
Britannia Works from the air. Marshall and Track Marshall occupied the top half of the old works. The buildings that once housed the wheeled tractor division were next to the car park in the centre of the picture. They have since been demolished and replaced by a Tesco supermarket.

The 'time being' was a remarkably short period of time! Within a week the majority of production personnel, together with many clerical, administrative, engineering, sales and service staff were told by the receivers that they were no longer required.

Then, as now, I was strong in the belief that we British should support our own industries and, whenever and wherever possible, should buy British-made products. So it did nothing to endear this team of receivers to me when each morning they arrived in the factory car park in their fleet of top-of-the-range four-wheel drive foreign cars with the word Quattro on the boot lid. The fact they were made in Germany just added insult to injury.

The redundancy programme implemented by the receivers soon meant that what for the previous three years had been the busy general office and operational hub for both Marshall Tractors and Track Marshall had suddenly become only a shadow of

TOP:
Marshall tractors leave the Gainsborough factory on 29 April 1986 en-route to Kane & McPherson, the firm's distributor/importer at Ballycastle in Northern Ireland. Business as usual then for me and Eric Hopkins, left. Just for the record, the tractors are, right to left, 802X (No.3127D), 702X (No.3119D), 804XL (No.2207B) and 802XL (No.3123D).

RIGHT:
Loading a batch of Scunthorpe-built Marshall tractors bound for Swedish distributor, Brorssons, with Ron Kettle, left, and other members of the Marshall team.

its former self. The majority of desks were now empty, files and paperwork left just where they had been when their occupants were told they were no longer required. Sadly, many of my good colleagues of many years' standing were no longer there.

For whatever reason, my own redundancy notice was not among the first batch to be issued and, together with Peter Blair and Dominic McClafferty, I was retained to maintain contact with the dealer networks at home and abroad. It fell to me to negotiate with the customer in Equador to accept the delayed dispatch of the tractors for which Ron Kettle had obtained the order, as Ron was sadly no longer with the firm.

Those six Marshall 702s did go to Equador and while many other orders for tractors were cancelled, some new ones did arrive on Peter Blair's desk. In the main these were met by the completion of tractors that had been on the production line at the time the receivers took over the running of the business.

The three of us in that large office tried to keep some semblance of normality in our dealings with customers, with whom we had built up close relationships going back many years. Working for a team of receivers was far from a normal business environment, but looking back it was an experience which I am not sorry to have had, but one I would not wish to repeat.

I don't believe they were as astute as they, themselves, thought they were or, indeed, as they should have been. Future events would be an indication of that. Be all that as it may, the skeleton sales staff of Peter, Dominic and myself were employed by the receivers for another three months. However, as the old saying goes, all good things must come to an end. If working for the receivers was temporarily a good thing, they made sure it would not go on for too long by handing me my redundancy notice on Christmas Eve 1985. One tractor door had very firmly been closed! Would another one open?

The receivers appointed to administer the handling of the Marshall business in September 1985 continued with that function through until the spring of the following year. Even now I still wonder what brought about that sorry state of affairs?

I have already mentioned the general malaise in the worldwide market that was being felt by tractor manufacturers, both big and small. Possibly that was a factor in the demise of Marshall. If so, it was a factor over which the company had little, if any, control.

But what about other factors over which it might have had some influence? The development costs of the six-cylinder-engined 100 Series models would have been considerable. Was that development programme justified so early in the life of the company?

The Leyland-based models, made better by Marshall, as the advertising slogan proclaimed, were well accepted in the market place and small but useful inroads were being made into the strongholds of our competitors. Would it have been better to continue to develop these to ensure their ongoing competitiveness? The XL gearbox went into production at a fairly early stage and did much to overcome the shortcomings, in terms of available ratios, of the otherwise excellent Leyland Synchro transmission.

At the time of the receivership there was a second version of the transmission under development. Had it gone into production it would have provided a really excellent change-on-the-move splitter arrangement and there was, of course, a big demand in the market place for that.

Leyland and then Marshall was probably the only manufacturer not offering a splitter gear of this type. What might it have meant in the way of incremental sales of the four-cylinder models if such a feature had been available at the time of the introduction of the 904XL in late 1984?

Did such a young but growing company really need a museum of the size and quality of the one that enhanced the premises so impressively? As good as it was, it can be said, in hindsight, that it was hardly essential to the early success of the tractor business.

Again, looking back, I have to wonder about other aspects of the operation prior to that black day, 25 September 1985.

Was it right for the company to become involved with the strawboard process and incur the hefty development costs of trying to bring it to fruition? It is very easy to ask these questions with the benefit of hindsight, but I do have to wonder whether there might still have been a tractor manufacturing presence in Gainsborough today had there been a longer period of concentration on two proven product lines only: the existing Track Marshall business and the new Leyland-based range of Marshall wheeled tractors. Perhaps the temptation to have a company that was running before it was walking should have been resisted.

Be all that as it may, the end of one particular era had come. A huge wealth of knowledgeable and experienced personnel were, in the main, welcomed with open arms by our competitors and the Marshall works in Gainsborough was ultimately destined to become just another site for a supermarket.

After I left my desk for the last time on Christmas Eve 1985, the team of receivers remained in charge for a few more months. There is little I can say about that period because I wasn't there to witness it. History records that the receivers did get more than a few expressions of interest in the business, mainly from UK parties, and one serious enquiry from the USA that, I believe came very close to success. Trantor Tractors had several discussions with the receivers but, again, as history records Marshall ended up in the hands of Scunthorpe-based Bentall Simplex, a company best known at that time for its range of grain-handling, storage and drying equipment.

And so it was that in the spring of 1986, Britannia Works in Gainsborough began

BELOW LEFT:
A proud moment as I hand over the first Marshall 100-4 off the Scunthorpe line, serial number 3076D, to Mr and Mrs John Torne from Rawcliffe Bridge, Yorks. Supplying agents Alf Kitching & Sons of Crowle, Lincs, ordered it on 18 August 1986 and took delivery on 19 August.

BELOW RIGHT:
This prototype IMT-based Marshall 174 was shown at the 1987 Royal Show but was shelved after an adverse reaction from the press and dealers.

to come back to some semblance of business life again and Marshall, now trading as Marshall Tractors, was back in business. Ron Kettle and I were offered jobs in the newly formed sales department and we set about making contact with dealers both in the UK and abroad. Taking into account the totally unexpected collapse of the previous company, the news of the rebirth received a mixed reception. This was not helped by the fact that there appeared to be no plans to restart manufacturing using the Gainsborough production line.

And then news filtered through that there was to be an auction sale of the contents of Britannia Works, including the machine tools and other assets that had previously been considered crucial to the production of tractors. Was there, even now, the small workforce wondered, a serious future for the Marshall range?

Following the sale came an announcement that the entire business was to be moved to the Bentall Simplex base in Scunthorpe and by June 1986 the transfer had started.

Previously occupied by British Steel, Bentall Simplex's Scunthorpe factory covered 25 acres and had more than enough space to house Marshall Tractors, including a much-modified production department and the parts operation. The supply of service parts would continue to be a very important part of the business for a long time to come. In the mid-1980s there were, at a conservative estimate, over 200,000 Nuffield, Leyland and Marshall tractors still in service around the world and they all needed spare parts from time to time.

The re-establishment of the business in Scunthorpe did give a much-needed boost to confidence and orders for new tractors, while not exactly flooding in, were obtained by Ron and myself in quantities sufficiently large to create a considerable lengthening of the delivery times.

One of the maxims often quoted by the new chairman, Paul Theakston, at impromptu meetings with both production and sales personnel, was 'If at first you don't succeed – you're sacked!'

How many times this was quoted to purchasing and production personnel is not on record, but it took some time to have a beneficial effect on delivery times.

BELOW LEFT:
Replacing the Marshall 904 in 1987, the 954XL used a turbo-charged Perkins A4.236T engine developing 95hp.

BELOW RIGHT:
Alfie Spencer of dealer Springmount Tractors came over for the 1988 Royal Show and joined me on the Marshall stand. The displayed included one of the new 125-4 models.

TOP:
A feature of the new Marshall 'Plus Factor' Field Marshall tractors was the ease with which operators could access the air filter via the flip-up front nose cone.

CENTRE:
The mid-range Marshall 'Plus Factor' tractors adopted the angular sheet metal styling first seen on the 100 Series models introduced in 1984.

RIGHT:
Marshall's 'Plus Factor' tractors used the same Sekura Explorer cab as their predecessors, albeit with a slightly up-dated instrument binnacle.

By this time, the Leyland factory at Bathgate had all but closed (it eventually closed in 1986) and this meant that the supply of the 98 Series engines, both four- and six-cylinder versions, could not go on for much longer. To enable production to continue it would be necessary to find a different engine supplier and there was no need to look further than Perkins for the replacements. Work was started on this project with the aim of having Perkins-engined tractors in production in time for the Royal Show of 1987. For the time being, however, it was business almost as usual with the Leyland-powered models developed in Bathgate and refined in Gainsborough.

Tractors continued to be exported to several of the old-established markets, including Sweden, Denmark, France and Italy. One or two new ones were opened up, including Portugal, which had not taken tractors since the Bathgate days. The Marshall 100-4 remained in production and seemed to increase in popularity, partly as a result of a pricing policy that was distinctly more aggressive than had been possible in Gainsborough.

Bentall Simplex and Marshall products were on display on a joint stand at the 1986 Royal Show. We even exhibited a Scunthorpe-built prototype tractor fitted with the upmarket Sekura Explorer cab and a bonnet line with more than a passing resemblance to that of the 100 Series. Lurking under the skin was the somewhat dubious mechanics of a 70hp skid-unit produced by IMT in Yugoslavia. It is worth mentioning at this stage that IMTs were being imported into the UK by a sister company in the Bentall Simplex group.

In my experience it has never been possible, in engineering terms, to make a silk purse out of a sow's ear and so it proved to be the case with this particular combination. It was, however, a useful exercise in collecting and collating public opinion which, together with input from the knowledgeable gentlemen of the agricultural press, was virtually universal in its opposition to the possibility of such a tractor being put into production, particularly if it was to carry the proud Marshall name!

It is often said that small is beautiful; while the Scunthorpe production facility was small it could hardly be described as beautiful, but what it lacked in visual appeal it more than made up for in its versatility.

Orders for one-off specifications, which larger organisations would have not even considered, were readily accepted and dealt with. One such order came from Mervyn Price, a loyal dealer in mid-Wales. Mervyn was working on a deal with a long-standing Nuffield, Leyland and Marshall customer who, as much as he respected the merits of the Leyland 98 Series engines, did not want his next new tractor to be fitted with a power unit that was going out of production.

Could we, he asked, build him a 125-4 tractor fitted with a Perkins Phaser engine? The directors decided that we could so this is exactly what our engineers ended up doing. John Carr of Weobley in Herefordshire duly became the proud owner of the only Perkins-powered Marshall 125-4 in existence.

The closure of what remained of British Leyland's Bathgate plant, that once state-of-the-art manufacturing complex mid-way between Edinburgh and Glasgow, brought about the end of production of what, on more than one occasion, I have described as probably the finest range of tractor engines ever – the Leyland 98 Series.

The gates to the huge Bathgate factory were finally padlocked shut some time during late 1986. I am not sure whether the Leyland 98 Series engine production line was scrapped following the closure, or if it was picked up in its entirety and put down in some foreign factory where it lived to fight another day.

Even in the late 1980s the four- and six-cylinder versions of the Leyland 98 Series engines were still perfectly acceptable technically and in terms of their performance. It was probably the second of these two attributes that would have made the range appealing to a Middle or Far Eastern manufacturing concern.

It wouldn't have been the first Bathgate product to find itself travelling down a foreign production line. Production of the Leyland 154, born out of the original BMC Mini tractor, was transferred to a factory at Izmir in Turkey. Several years later it was moved to India, where a company known as Auto Tractors may still be producing it today, although I can't be sure about that. Certainly up until a few years ago they were still manufacturing the 1.5-litre diesel engine of BMC design which powered the 154.

TOP:
The popular four-wheel drive Marshall 854XL was powered by a Perkins four-cylinder turbo engine producing 85hp.

RIGHT:
Marshall 132, 100-4 and 125-4 tractors can be seen in the showroom of our Italian distributor, Agritractor of Marene, in either 1988 or 1989.

So, back in Scunthorpe, there was no option but to say a sad goodbye to the Leyland 98 Series engines and an enthusiastic hello to Perkins. As I have already mentioned, the plan was to have Perkins-engined tractors in production in time for a public launch at the 1987 Royal Show, which is exactly what happened. The installation of the Perkins engine was not the major problem it might have been in competitive tractors of different configurations.

The four-cylinder Perkins 4.236 power unit sat very neatly within the cast side members of the massive main frame which was first seen in the original Nuffield tractor of 1948. The 1987 version of the frame, while longer and deeper in its proportions, still bore a close resemblance to its original predecessor of 40 or so years earlier. From a totally biased standpoint I would have to say that this speaks volumes for the precision and forethought that went into the original design of the first Nuffield tractors. In many ways, the engine installation was the easy bit, although Jonathon Holt, the engineer who had the main responsibility for the programme, would probably not agree with that.

It was decided that three new models of 75hp, 85hp and 95hp would be introduced, all using the Perkins 4.236 engine. In the interests of keeping manufacturing complexity to a minimum, it was also decided that all models, whether two- or four-wheel drive, would have the longer wheel base provided by the XL creep speed gearbox, irrespective of whether the creep speed mechanicals were fitted or not. A larger, heavier-duty Laycock clutch was specified together with an uprated four-star rear axle differential.

Several other detail changes were also specified, the most important of which was a considerable increase in the capacity of the front-mounted fuel tank, which in production versions would take 30 gallons. Cynics of the time would doubtless claim that a larger tank was necessary now that we were employing the more thirsty horses bred in Peterborough!

Granted, the Bathgate-built Leyland 4/98 engines had left behind a formidable reputation for miserly fuel consumption, but the Perkins 4.236 was still of a relatively long stroke configuration and we were confident that when it came to gallons per horsepower/hour it would continue to be more than a match for its over-square and short-stoke competitors.

All these items of new specification continued to be topped off by the proven and market-leading Explorer quiet cab. Forward of this it was necessary to create a new bonnet line; all Leyland-engined tractors, whether they were produced at Bathgate, Gainsborough or Scunthorpe, had been fitted with the original Leyland design introduced in late 1969 when the Nuffield marque gave way to Leyland.

With the introduction of the Perkins engines and new ancillaries, including the larger fuel tank and increased radiator dimensions, it was necessary to develop a new shape and with it a new image to help market what were, in effect, very different tractors to anything that had gone before. A design of styling based on that developed for the Marshall 100 Series models was the obvious and automatic choice. Within the Bentall Simplex complex at Scunthorpe there were ample facilities to produce the straight-edged and angular design of bonnet-work that had proved so acceptable on the six-cylinder Gainsborough-built tractors.

Several prototype kits were produced, changed and refined before the design was deemed acceptable by the directors and allowed to go into production. In a relatively small, privately-run company where owners and directors could, when necessary, adopt a hands-on approach, it was quite remarkable how quickly things could happen on occasions. Perhaps not always with the finest of attention to detail that so characterised the design and development processes in Bathgate and to a lesser degree in Gainsborough, but things could get done, particularly when the chairman was not unaccustomed to showing a degree of impatience.

An aspect of new tractor development that is rarely, if ever, given prominence is the work that has to be done to ensure compliance with various rules, regulations and the law. It was not necessary to have the new models with their Perkins engines cab-tested for crush and impact. This was because in terms of total weight and dimensions they were very similar to the XL models with Leyland engines produced in Gainsborough that had been tested at the NIAE at Silsoe a few years earlier. The new tractors did, however, have to be sent to Silsoe for in-cab noise tests, happily they received approval, with noise levels very similar to their Leyland-engined predecessors.

So everything was in place for the first public showing at the 1987 Royal Show. Press advertising either side of the show proclaimed the new models as the New Field Marshalls and the New Mid Range Plus Factor Tractors.

The copy from one advert read: 'There are three new horsepowers and nine new models in the new Marshall mid-range of two- and four-wheel drive tractors. Marshalls have been engineering and producing agricultural equipment longer than most other household names in the tractor business and the new Plus Factor tractors exhibit all the hallmarks of the experience gained over more than 140 years. These new Marshalls

Here I am with fellow Marshall sales manager Ron Kettle and the first badge-engineered Marshall 264 compact tractor.

are first and foremost the result of a carefully arranged marriage. A marriage between what is acknowledged as being the best tractor transmission in the business – the Marshall Synchro – and a range of four-cylinder engines from Perkins, the world's finest manufacturer of tractor diesels.'

The three new power ranges mentioned earlier resulted in model designations of 752X and 754X, 852X and 854X, with the availability of the creep speed XL option in each case and, at the top of the range, the 954XL.

The weather during the 1987 Royal Show was sunny and warm, the type that made the long days of stand duty bearable and almost a pleasure. The Marshall stand was manned by Ron Kettle, Martin Stokes and myself, not a large team but, I like to think, a reasonably capable one. There was also a new member, Barry Wood, who had been employed to specialise in the sale of another new model, the mechanics of which bore more than a passing resemblance to those of the aged design of the Massey Ferguson 35, but more of this later.

On this occasion, it was possible to report that the reaction to the real Marshall models with their Perkins engines, from the public and also from the gentlemen of the press, was every bit as warm as the weather at the 1987 Royal.

Earlier I mentioned Marshall Tractors' attempt to marry the mechanical wet bits of a 70hp Yugoslavian skid unit produced by IMT to the excellent Leyland/Marshall Explorer cab, the result of which was exhibited at the 1986 Royal Show.

This one-off unit was, to put it mildly, not well received by the general farming public and even less well so by the agricultural press. At that time another company within the Bentall Simplex Group had the sole UK import rights for the IMT range. Prior to this arrangement, I think I am correct in saying that IMT had its own import arrangement in this country, albeit a fairly low-key affair that met with only limited success.

To those not acquainted with all the details of the IMT product, which, in my view, never bore too close an examination, their lack of UK success may seem surprising bearing in mind that their design was based on ageing but nevertheless well-proven Massey Ferguson designs. The most popular model of the IMT range, the 539, appeared to be an almost exact replica of the Ferguson 35. However, the advantages conferred upon it by its illustrious forebear were almost completely negated by its adoptive parentage. Quality control as part of the manufacturing process appeared to be an unknown function in IMT's vast state-owned assembly plant in Belgrade, Yugoslavia.

THE FIELD MARSHALLS

MODEL	CONFIGURATION	CYLINDERS	POWER	TRANSMISSION
752X	2WD	4	74hp	9F/3R
752XL	2WD	4	74hp	15F/5R
754X	4WD	4	74hp	9F/3
754XL	4WD	4	74hp	15F/5R
852X	2WD	4T	85hp	9F/3R
852XL	2WD	4T	85hp	15F/5R
854X	4WD	4T	85hp	9F/3R
854XL	4WD	4T	85hp	15F/5R
954XL	4WD	4T	94hp	15F/5R

However, nothing ventured, nothing gained. In spite of the adverse public reaction to the Marshall 174 exhibited at the 1986 Royal Show, it was decided to go down a similar route using the IMT 539 as a base for a smaller Marshall tractor. From the point of view of building up a range there was some sound logic in this. Below the 75hp Perkins-engined 752 and 754 there was, in the early Scunthorpe days, nothing to replace the 25hp Leyland 154 or its Turkish-built successor, the 30hp Leyland 302.

The Marshall 132 was introduced as the first serious result of a programme of badge engineering. It was based on the IMT 539 skid unit and came with a Duncan quiet cab.

The Marshall 132 was first shown during the week of the 1986 Royal Smithfield Show in a private room at an upmarket hotel close to Earls Court, the company having been unable to get stand space inside the exhibition.

Determined that this new model should not miss out on all the publicity surrounding the annual Smithfield event, the company invited its dealers, the press and the farming public to the nearby Tara Hotel. The arrangement worked well, although for Ron Kettle and myself it was a marked contrast to the day-long, non-stop buzz of working on a large stand inside the main exhibition.

The Marshall 132 gave every appearance of being a neat, well-balanced and not unattractive small tractor. While showing its obvious Ferguson parentage it was, in terms of its cosmetic appearance and detail finish, far removed from its close IMT stablemate. At least this is how it came across in the refined surroundings of the Tara Hotel. Whether in the field it was going to be possible sell it as a Marshall silk purse rather than a sow's ear from IMT remained to be seen.

In the event, the 132 sold mainly to that sector of the market where the BMC Mini and its various derivatives, right up to the Turkish-built Marshall 302, had been so successful. Whether they were ultimately a commercial success is another matter, especially after the amount of work that went into making sure the skid units had an acceptable degree of reliability.

The launch of the Marshall 132 by the Scunthorpe-based company was followed by a programme of further product diversification. The chairman, aware of the growing market for compact tractors, asked me to make contact with Ferrari, an Italian manufacturer of compact tractors. Following an initial exchange of correspondence by telex and fax (this was in the pre-email era) Frank Theakston, purchasing manager Keith Farmer, and I visited the Ferrari factory in northern Italy. Out of this meeting came an agreement whereby Marshall would import and distribute the Ferrari's 18hp and 26hp models, which would be sold in Marshall Harvest Gold colours and badged as Marshalls.

Even in the late 1980s this was far from being an unusual procedure: Ford, Massey Ferguson and John Deere had all set up sales and marketing arrangements with Japanese manufacturers of compact tractors and in many cases these are still in existence today.

In Italy the standard colour of Ferrari tractors was lime green but tractors destined for Marshall arrived in Scunthorpe ready painted in Marshall Harvest Gold with white wheels. All that was necessary prior to shipment out to the dealers, apart from the standard PDI, was to add Marshall decals and the small cast Field Marshall badge to the front grille.

In common with established model numbering patterns, the 18hp tractor was designated the 184 (18hp/4WD) and the 26hp model was the 264 (26hp/4WD). Both tractors were ruggedly built with heavy castings for the gearbox, rear axles and hydraulic casing, and a substantial pressed chassis in which the engines were mounted. In many ways they were more robust than their Japanese counterparts. Both had air-cooled power units under the bonnet; the 184 had a twin-cylinder Ruggerini and the 264 had a Lombardini engine, again with two cylinders. That these tractors performed well was beyond dispute, but neither could claim to be among the quietest compacts in the market place. It took some long time to get this through to Ferrari, so much so that one wag at Scunthorpe commented that perhaps they had become deaf after working so long with their small, high-speed, two-cylinder, air-cooled diesels.

In the fullness of time the message was pushed home and in due course the 264, which was the better seller of the two, became available with a three-cylinder Lombardini engine, which this time was water-cooled.

So with the introduction of the Marshall 132 (I cannot recall how this model designation was arrived at, but it definitely did not fit in with the established Marshall formula of power and the number of driven wheels) together with the 184 and 264 compacts, a programme of model and range diversification appeared to have been put in hand.

Further contacts were made with Italian companies. Frank Theakston and I even visited the Merlo factory to discuss the possibility of a marketing agreement for their range of telehandlers. At that time they were not selling in the UK, but neither were they enthusiastic about the idea of having another name (Marshall) on their products.

Two other admittedly much smaller companies were more interested in selling into the UK and didn't object to the Marshall name being on their products. The first of these was the manufacturer of a small two-wheel drive quad-bike, which was given the name Scout. From memory only two were brought into the country for assessment purposes and it was fairly soon decided that with its small, air-cooled Piaggio engine

BELOW LEFT:
The photo-shoot for the Marshall 184 took place in the picturesque grounds of Normanby Hall, Scunthorpe.

BELOW RIGHT:
Marshall's IMT-based 132 was unveiled to the press and dealer network at the Tara Hotel in London in December 1986.

and rear-wheel drive only, it was not going to be a match for the growing number of mainly Japanese-built bikes. A leaflet was produced but the Scout was quietly dropped from the range at a fairly early stage.

The second, dubbed the Ranger, came from another small Italian company, which specialised in the design and manufacture of small four-wheel drive load carriers. As with the Ferrari-based compacts, the Ranger came into this country painted in Harvest Gold, with four-wheel drive as standard, a three-seater cab and a tipping rear body. Golf courses and the like were seen as potential customers, along with market gardens, garden centres, caravan parks and the leisure industry in general.

The Ranger was also fitted with the aforementioned Ruggerini two-cylinder, air-cooled diesel engine, which, although enclosed in a compartment, still made its presence known to the driver and passengers. Once it had undergone certain refinements at the hands of production personnel in Scunthorpe, the Ranger became a reasonably acceptable little product and one that, had time allowed, could have been sold in reasonable numbers, but that is another story.

Back home in Scunthorpe, one other small product development programme was coming to fruition, this time involving the largest tractor in the range, the 100-4.

Sales of the relatively new 100-4 tractor were pretty good through 1986 and into 1987 and to maintain the momentum a more powerful version was introduced. This continued to make use of that great tractor diesel, the long-stroke, slow-revving Leyland 6/98, which was turbo-charged to produce the extra power. It involved the minimum of change to important engine ancillaries, such as cooling, and no change at all to anything from the clutch back. It was a simple, low-cost exercise and increased the rated power of the Marshall 100-4 from 103hp to 125hp. With that increase the 125-4 became the most powerful Marshall tractor to date.

With a range now extending from 18hp up to 125hp, what other developments were in the pipeline? I continued to accompany Frank Theakston to shows and exhibitions in Italy and also to the SIMA show in Paris. Might there, we wondered, be other Continental manufacturers interested in changing the colour of a proportion of their production to Harvest Gold and allowing it to carry the name Marshall?

Sales leaflets for the Marshall Scout quad-bike, Ranger 4x4 vehicle and 184 and 264 compact tractors. The Scout and Ranger came and went, but we did sell a decent number of compacts.

Twelve
Austrian Adventure

During my previous jottings I have made reference to the badge-engineering arrangement that existed between Scunthorpe-based Marshall Tractors and Ferrari, the Italian manufacturer of compact tractors.

This was not the first time that the famous and much respected name of Marshall had been applied to a foreign-built product. That probably occurred when the Gainsborough-based company began to import the 302, a development of the original BMC Mini, which was built by the Turkish company BMC Sinayi at their Izmir factory.

The process of applying the brand name of one company to the product of another was far from a new concept, even in the 1980s. As long ago as the early 1960s, when I first joined the Nuffield tractor division of what was then the British Motor Corporation, the same procedure was being applied. I suppose in today's parlance it might be described as a marketing tool, used to extend the already considerable range of automotive products manufactured by that once mighty company. The procedure came to be known as badge engineering and, in the early days, was rather looked down upon by certain sections of the industry and by self-appointed experts of the specialist press.

To move away from things agricultural for a moment, it is worth remembering that the original Mini car, designed by Alec Issigonis and still renowned throughout the world today, was badge engineered. It should not be confused with the present-day BMW product (even the German car manufacturing giant was unable to find a better name).

We tend to forget that the Mini was also included in the ranges of Wolseley and Riley – upmarket brand names which are sadly slipping from the memory of so many in this country. The Wolseley version of the Mini was known as the Hornet and the Riley version was called the Elf.

A whole range of models was developed out of the Farina-styled Morris Oxford and Austin Cambridge of the 1960s and out of the Morris/Austin 1100/1300 range to provide basically similar cars that carried such famous names as Wolseley and Riley, plus MG and Vanden Plas.

TOP:
Steyr of Austria was the market leader in its home market and the size of its stand at the 1990 Linz Agricultural Machinery Exhibition reflected its dominant position.

CENTRE:
This 8085 Turbo (72hp) model formed part of a large display of Steyr tractors at the 1990 Linz Agricultural Machinery Exhibition.

RIGHT:
A group of Marshall dealers toured Steyr's St. Valentin factory in Austria in 1991, from left, Robin Sharp, unknown, David Lowe and Robin Sharp junior.

The Morris and Austin models werc regarded as the bread-and-butter, standard versions of the range. The other four marques, with different front grilles, styling modifications, increasingly high levels of interior trim and finish, and mechanical changes to provide higher levels of performance, provided standards of comfort and opulence which would appeal to customers who wanted just that. At BMC, badge engineering was largely to do with the economies of scale – one basic bodyshell provided as wide a range as possible, to the benefit of the distribution network and the market place.

The concept of badge engineering was, and probably still is, relatively common within the tractor industry. I seem to recall that Ford, Massey Ferguson and John Deere to name but a few have all applied their names to Japanese-built compact tractors.

What about other items of agricultural equipment? It may almost be forgotten now, but it is worth remembering that the first ploughs imported into this country from Norway were sold not in the red and green of Kverneland, but were painted yellow and marketed under the famous Bamfords of Uttoxeter name. At about the same time, the Jones baler company based in North Wales produced mechanically identical pick-up balers, one painted red with their own name on it and one painted orange carrying the Allis-Chalmers name. It was badge engineering pure and simple.

There are other examples, including, again at Uttoxeter, Bamfords' dalliance in the combine harvester business with first Volvo and then Laverda. Another good example is Bomford's highly successful Superflow chisel plough, which was sold by Massey Ferguson as the 24 model for most of the 1960s and 70s. There have been countless other examples of badge engineering over the years.

Returning to Marshall Tractors at Scunthorpe, my boss in the late 1980s, Frank Theakston, was involved in the grain drying and handling side of the Bentall Simplex business. He was keen to expand his understanding of the tractor business as a whole and of the European situation in particular. Frank and I made regular trips to the major agricultural machinery exhibitions in France and Italy. While there we had both impromptu and formal meetings with numerous companies; I have already mentioned Merlo and its range of telehandlers but I also remember discussions with Goldoni from Italy and Schluter, the German manufacturer of specialist, high-horsepower tractors. Frank was keen to sound out such companies and to get a feel for their attitude towards what might be, in effect, a badge engineering arrangement.

At the SIMA exhibition in Paris in the spring of 1988 we were surprised to come across quite a large and prestigious stand with numerous red and white tractors carrying the name Steyr. I had to admit to Frank that after more than 20 years in the tractor business I knew very little about Steyr of Austria or its products. I knew that at various times from the late 1960s onwards the company had attempted to sell its tractors in the UK, ultimately with little success, but that was about it.

I recall that we spent quite a long time on the stand examining the products and assessing the amount of interest being shown in them by the multi-national visitors to this huge exhibition which, in terms of size, dwarfed London's Royal Smithfield Show.

I remember Frank asking for a quick assessment and I recall listing to him three negative aspects of the Steyr design – dry drum brakes, quiet cabs that were rigidly mounted and a comparatively small engine capacity for the quoted horsepowers.

The flip side of this was that the engines were of my much-preferred long stroke configuration. Apart from the minus points, Frank and I agreed that there appeared to be a neatness of general design and level of finish that gave the impression that here was perhaps a product of some quality.

Having spent 30 minutes or so on the stand, Frank and I remarked to each other that it was surprising that no member of the Steyr staff had made any effort to do a selling job on us, to offer us brochures or even to acknowledge our interest in any other way.

How different to the way that Nuffield, Leyland and Marshall personnel, both sales and service, had been schooled over the years. Visitors to our stands were usually always greeted by a company representative and, in the case of farmers and prospective dealers, the noting of names and addresses was obligatory. The likes of Alan Hawes, Ray Runciman, Mike Keogh, Brian Webb and many others were past masters at this and, without doubt, many additional sales were made as a result.

Back on the Steyr stand, however, the approach appeared much more laid back; if you wanted help or information, you had to ask for it! Bob Turner, sales director during the late Nuffield/early Leyland days, would have had their guts for garters.

Frank was sufficiently interested in the product and asked that I make our presence known, which I duly did. We were politely offered refreshment, although there was still no real attempt to establish the nature of our interest. It was left to Frank to volunteer the information that we were looking for a supplier of skid units (engine, clutch, transmission and hydraulic unit) on to which we, in Scunthorpe, could engineer our own bonnet work and cab. The Leyland/Marshall Explorer cab was in a different league to that being shown on the Steyr stand.

It was also explained that if an agreement could be reached the resulting tractors would be marketed in the UK under the name Marshall. We were asked about horse-power mix, specifications and quantities. Only then did a glimmer of interest begin to become apparent. Having been trained through the BMC/British Leyland system, I found the Steyr approach puzzling and lacking in good business understanding. This feeling was confirmed during the following weeks when several promised deadline dates for the receipt of faxed pricing information were not met.

In the event, all this proved to be of no great importance. In Scunthorpe changes at the top were taking place. We found ourselves with a new chairman whose background was in accountancy. He was not keen on the economics of building Perkins-engined mid-range models in relatively small volumes, or on the idea of importing Austrian-built skid units on which we could mount the Danish-built Explorer cab.

He was, of course, aware of the contact with Steyr and decided to go and see for himself, by himself, what it was all about. On his return he announced that a new company would be formed, still based in Scunthorpe, which would import and distribute a range of Steyr tractors throughout the UK and Ireland, badge engineered as Marshalls.

Apart from anything else, this sounded like the death-knell of the original Nuffield, Leyland and Marshall design of mid-range tractors. What was it I said earlier about accountants?

TOP:
Badge engineering wasn't new to me because my previous employer, the British Motor Corporation, used the concept to turn the Morris/Austin 1100 into an upmarket Riley Kestrel.

CENTRE:
Marshall – the future! Nottingham University was the venue for Marshall's unveiling of its new D-Series tractors, badge-engineered from Steyr of Austria.

LEFT:
With its ample floor area and large presentation screen, Nottingham University made a perfect launch venue for the Marshall D-Series tractors.

In their home country of Austria, Steyr tractors were, back in the late 1980s and early 90s, a huge force to be reckoned with. Their range was extensive in terms of horsepower coverage and they were achieving sales leadership with a massive share of their own home tractor market.

On the part of the Austrian farmers, industrial users and local authorities there seemed to be a desire to buy the product, mainly because it was very good and because it was built in their own country. This, even then, was in contrast to the UK, where farmers were not averse to buying from abroad.

It is too late now for the once great UK tractor manufacturing industry to benefit from that type of attitude, but if farmers in Austria could do it, and probably still do, why couldn't a similar attitude have applied in this country? The UK, after all, used to produce more tractors than the rest of the world put together, 75-80% of which would have been exported, making a massive contribution to the balance of payments. The tractor manufacturing industry in this country used to provide high levels of employment and in doing so created meaningful, productive jobs of genuine quality of the type that are now in such short supply in this call-centre economy of ours.

Be all that as it may, the new chairman of the Scunthorpe-based Marshall company had returned from his meeting with Steyr at the St. Valentin factory with an agreement to market across the UK and Ireland a selected range of tractors that would be badge-engineered as Marshalls. This meeting would have been some time around the middle of 1988.

Steyr tractors were marketed world-wide by a company known as Steyr Land-maschinen-technik, which was part of a holding company registered as Steyr-Daimler-Puch AG. The Daimler part of this name had an appeal in certain sections of the Scunthorpe headquarters and it was decided that the new company formed to import the Steyr/Marshall tractors should trade as Marshall Daimler Ltd, and this was the name that was duly registered.

It was also decided, in conjunction with the management of Steyr, that the Royal Smithfield Show of 1989 should be the event where the important marketing arrangement was officially made public. Additionally, it was agreed that the all-important

BELOW LEFT:
Steyr had a number of specially prepared tractors that it used for exhibition purposes and they were usually badged 'Steyr Exclusive'. This one was the source of much curiosity at our Nottingham D-Series launch.

BELOW RIGHT:
The metallic purple Marshall 'Exclusive' took centre stage at the Nottingham launch. I can be seen far right explaining the features of the new tractors to our dealers.

distributor/dealer launch should be held just before the show, in late October or early November.

Prior to this Marshall sales and service staff had to undergo product instruction and familiarisation courses at Steyr's St. Valentin training school. Also to be agreed were final specifications of the models at seven different horsepower levels between 60hp and 150hp, which would form the new Marshall range.

Steyr tractors, as they came off the St Valentin production line, were finished in a red and white colour scheme with a black skid unit. It had already been agreed that tractors destined for Marshall at Scunthorpe would be despatched in the standard Marshall colours of Harvest Gold and black.

During a visit to the factory in early summer 1989, Andy McMeechan, Martin Stokes and I, together with our recently appointed managing director, Peter Carter, saw the first tractors to be finished in Marshall colours leave the production line. The St Valentin factory wasn't huge but it had an atmosphere of quality, attention to detail and extreme cleanliness. The workers also took a great pride in the manufacture of each and all of its products.

There was considerable interest on the part of the assembly workers in these first Harvest Gold tractors, even more so when we began to apply the Marshall decals and the famous Field Marshall badge to the front of the bonnet. On future tractors these items would be fitted in Scunthorpe, but on the first units we took the decals and badges with us to St. Valentin. This was to enable the first tractors to be taken directly to a nearby studio so that photographic work could be carried out to allow the production of the sales brochures to begin.

The work was done by an Austrian photographer used by Steyr but who worked under the direction of our own in-house specialist in literature design. He had finished provisional layouts prior to leaving for Austria and I had also mapped out much of the accompanying text that I wanted to have checked by the Steyr product specialists to ensure technical accuracy. We were, after all, adopting a completely new product range and after nearly 30 years living and breathing its predecessor were on a very steep learning curve.

The models which were to form the new Marshall range provided horsepowers of 64, 72, 80, 90, 110, 135 and 150. In Scunthorpe we considered that the Steyr pattern of model numbering was not particularly appropriate to the UK and Irish markets and, in any case, it was policy to Marshallise the tractors as much as possible. Part of the marketing policy was to ensure that, as with past Nuffield, Leyland and Marshall tractors, the model designation provided an indication of horsepower and whether a particular tractor was two or four-wheel drive.

As an example of this, the model that Steyr called the 8110 became the Marshall D944 because it was in the 90hp category and it was four-wheel drive. The Steyr 8085, which was in the 70hp bracket, became either the D742 or D744 according to whether it was two- or four-wheel drive.

In other words the last digit would normally indicate two- or four-wheel drive and the preceding ones a close approximation of horsepower.

So what, you might ask, was the significance of the 'D' before each model number?

Well, as mentioned earlier, the company created to market the Steyr-based Marshall range was Marshall Daimler Ltd. There was a suggestion that the word Daimler should appear on the bonnet side panels along with Marshall. There was also an indication that Jaguar Daimler (as in the manufacturer of the famous cars with those names) were not over-enthusiastic about this!

We decided not to use the word Daimler on the tractors, but it was signified by the letter D in the model name. With this move, the new range became known as the Marshall D Series.

The Scunthorpe team had no qualms about the association with the Daimler name. Everything we had seen and learnt in St Valentin, and everything we came to know about its products, led us to believe that in terms of quality, reliability and durability here was a product that compared well with Nuffield in its Ward End days, and also with the Gainsborough-built Marshalls. To emphasise this, all aspects of the marketing support package were produced to the highest standard possible; the literature was tip-top and the introduction of the new range to the trade matched this in every respect.

The distributor and dealer launch was held in the autumn of 1989 on the campus of Nottingham University and the presentation took place in one of their superb lecture theatres. We did have one little hiccup on the day prior to the launch, when it was discovered that the tractors were too high to be driven through the double doors and on to the stage. We overcame this by deflating the rear tyres, following which the ever-resourceful Martin Stokes set about reinflating them using a compressor from the boot of his company car.

A metallic purple tractor, the Marshall Exclusive, formed the centrepiece of a hidden-from-view display of three tractors on a sunken stage, accompanied by a D642 and a D844.

Delegates to the launch entered the theatre to the soft tones of 'Tales from the Vienna Woods' and, at a predetermined time, spotlights came on and the three tractors were ceremoniously unveiled. An explanation of the new company, its structure and

BELOW LEFT:
The name on the bonnet said Marshall but the D-Series look was pure Steyr.

BELOW RIGHT:
The flagship D-150 model (150hp) gave Marshall access to a completely new sector of the market.

its aims was given by the newly appointed Peter Carter of Marshall Daimler Ltd, while Steyr export sales manager Peter Zimpel spoke in immaculate English about his company and its already good relationship with Marshall.

My own part in this was to talk about the new range, its specification and technicalities, and how it compared with the competition. All the time on the screen at the rear of the stage was the slogan 'Marshall – the future'.

From a stage management point of view the presentation was flawless and as it ended the dealers were invited on to the stage for a close inspection of the three tractors and of others which completed the range lined up in an adjacent display area. It was generally agreed that the product looked good and that its specification was competitive. Some regretted the loss of the Leyland/Marshall Explorer cab and others expressed concern at the specification of the brakes – for example, there were no oil-immersed systems below 135hp.

Other dealers, realising the sales potential of the new range, saw things from a different point of view. What would be the attitude of the other franchises they represented – Same and Deutz-Fahr, in particular – if they now began to involve themselves in a truly competitive Marshall franchise which also had the backing and support of a company the size of Steyr?

If this was to be the future, what about the past? What about that long and illustrious, if not a little chequered, history of Nuffield and Leyland tractors and the variants known as Marshall that owed so much to the original design which had stood the test of time over the preceding 40 years? What about some of the dealers present on that day in Nottingham, who had built successful businesses, in part, on the strengths of those tractors?

It had to be explained how the Nuffield/Leyland design had reached the end of the production line and that it was, indeed, a thing of the past. Business people can't afford to be sentimental and although there was some sentimentality expressed on that first day of November 1989, there wasn't a lot.

THE MARSHALL D-SERIES

MODEL	DRIVE	HP	CYLINDERS	UNITS SOLD
D-544	4WD	54	3	0
D-642	2WD	64	4	3
D-644	4WD	64	4	2
D-742	2WD	72	4	3
D-744	4WD	72	4	1
D-842	2WD	80	4	2
D-844	4WD	80	4	22
D-944	4WD	90	6	15
D-110	4WD	110	6T	19
D-135	4WD	135	6T	1
D-150	4WD	150	6T	0
S-544	4WD	54	3	1
S-644	4WD	64	4	1
S-744	4WD	72	4	2

NB: 1st tractor delivered 8/1/1990; last tractor delivered 16/8/1991

Today, I don't mind admitting that I am a bit of a sentimentalist. Looking back nearly 20 years now it seems a little sad that the end of the tractor design that took its original name from the home village in Oxfordshire of Sir William Morris, later Lord Nuffield, should have been accepted in such an uncomplaining and resigned manner.

At the 1989 Royal Smithfield Show, the newly formed Marshall Daimler company proudly presented its new range of Marshall tractors made not in Gainsborough or Scunthorpe, but several hundred miles away in the St. Valentin factory of Steyr Landmaschinentechnik. As a matter of interest, St. Valentin is on the outskirts of the picturesque town of Steyr from which, of course, the company and the tractors take their name.

The 1989 Royal Smithfield Show was a busy one. Space was at a premium and because we had missed several shows during the late 1980s we had to take what was available. What was offered and what was taken was a well-placed stand on the first floor.

It might not have been our first choice but we made up for any disadvantage by ensuring that the design of the stand was spot on. So much so that the Steyr executives who were with us for most of the week took the design back to St. Valentin so that they could replicate it at regional shows in Austria.

Martin Stokes, Andy MacMeechan, Andy Lambert and myself, together with Marshall Daimler's managing director, Peter Carter, were kept busy enough on the stand. There was some genuine farmer interest in the new range, yet there was an equal amount of critical comment that the previous Nuffield/Leyland-based models were no longer available.

There was nothing complicated about the model numbering system: the first two numbers indicated the approximate power and the last number the axle configuration, i.e. two-wheel or four-wheel drive. Hence the D642 was 62hp and two-wheel drive.

Such criticism came, in the main, from operators who had rarely, if ever, purchased the product and I was left to ponder that had they done so, then it might still have been in production and on show at Smithfield 1989. The interest was probably borne out of the obvious visual quality of the tractors on show. Build quality and finish came right at the top of the production priority list in St. Valentin and this was quite obvious on visual inspection, which was about all that was possible at Earls Court.

The Harvest Gold finish on our show tractors was of the highest order and it played quite a big part in helping to impress upon visitors to the stand that they were looking at a quality product. Not everybody would agree with me, but I was of the opinion that the tractors looked much smarter in the Marshall colours than Steyr's traditional red and white.

Be all that as it may, I said earlier how it is odd that history repeats itself. In terms of engine specification it did, indeed, repeat itself, to some degree, at least. You will by now know of my affection for the last of the Bathgate-produced Leyland tractor engines – the 98 Series with its long-stroke configuration. Well, here we were, back in 1989 and going into 1990 and many of the majors such as Ford, John Deere and Fiat were still trying to extol the benefits of over-square, short-stroke engines. Yet with the Marshall D Series we were able to continue our love affair with long-stroke power units and with all the benefits these offered in terms of low-revving fuel economy and extended working life.

Not that the Steyr engine had the same chart-topping bore-to-stroke ratio provided by the 4/98 and 6/98 Leyland power units, but they were still pretty good and in the field it was possible to demonstrate this feature to very good effect.

To continue the specification comparisons a little further, the standard Steyr gearbox of the day provided a synchromesh transmission with 16 forward and eight reverse ratios, which put it in a rather higher league than the well-respected Leyland Synchro transmission designed in the mid-1970s by Mike Barnes and Simon Evans.

Some might point out, however, that with the introduction of the Marshall designed XL option, the Synchro box did have 15 forward and five reverse ratios. Neither Leyland nor Marshall ever had a change-on-the-go splitter arrangement, not, that is, until the arrival of the D Series. These tractors had a splitter called D-Matic which was operated via a switch set into the top of the main gear lever.

On paper, at least, the braking specification for the new D Series Marshalls did not compare with that of their British-built predecessors. The latter, of course, had Girling multi-plate oil-immersed discs that had become just about the worldwide benchmark for tractor braking systems.

Surprisingly, St. Valentin-built tractors still relied on either dry drums or external dry disc and caliper types, depending on horsepower.

In terms of its lift capacity, the D Series really was ahead of the range it was replacing. The four-cylinder models were good but not exceptional at 2626kg, but the 90hp D-944 and the 110hp D-110 would lift 4772kg and 5845kg respectively, and were right at the top of the 1990 league in this regard.

Overall, the D Series tractors were good and would bear comparison with anything from other major, market-leading manufacturers. The Marshall team came away from the 1989 Royal Smithfield Show not exactly ecstatic but very happy with the reaction received both from farmers and some potential new dealers.

Some of the older-established dealers, however, were not as forthcoming and it wasn't long into 1990 before we began to receive indications they did not feel able to continue to represent Marshall. Whether this was as a result of pressure from other manufacturers they also represented, or a decision of their own making that the new Marshalls were now so similar in terms of specification to the tractors from those other franchises, we shall never know.

I believe there was an element of both factors involved but, nevertheless the loss of several of our top-performing dealers was a severe blow, and perhaps one that Marshall Daimler didn't expect and for which those within the company who had control of the purse strings were not prepared. In spite of this early set-back, sales of the D Series made steady progress during 1990 and while numbers were not sufficient to register on the monthly issue of national registration figures, the four-wheel drive 844, 944 and 110 models began to find customers.

Two new Irish dealers, Timothy McFarland in the north and Springmount Tractors in Eire, were introduced to the range and they began to take tractors on a regular basis.

Robin Sharpe at Alresford in Hampshire and J. Charnley & Sons from near Chorley in Lancashire were also active in promoting the sale of the D Series. In mid-Wales, Mervyn Price used 944 and 110 tractors in his own contracting fleet of Leyland and Marshall tractors and the exposure this provided resulted in the sale of numerous D Series models.

In Scotland, Marrs of Burrelton, who previously had been very successful in importing Steyrs direct from the manufacturer and had accepted the change a little reluctantly but with very good grace, also began to sell Harvest Gold tractors. David Tunstall of Tunstall Tractors Ltd from Kirkby Stephen in Cumbria was quick to recognise and appreciate the competitive strengths of the D Series. During that first year he probably sold as many tractors, if not more, than any other Marshall dealer. It is a fact that Peter Zimpel, Steyr's export sales manager, was not unhappy with the volume of Harvest Gold tractors leaving the factory gates in St. Valentin during 1990. Certainly, the numbers represented a massive increase over what they had been selling into the UK and Eire markets previously.

There were, however, several dark clouds on the horizon: the UK market for tractors was becoming increasingly price competitive again and discounting by the major manufacturers was rife. Price, as we know, is all important. Additionally, the prices agreed with Steyr when the contract was first set up by our chairman, while probably the best they could offer, did not help dealers make the D Series as competitive as they should have been in the early stages of the launch period. On top of this, exchange rates between the £sterling and the Austrian schilling were moving in the wrong direction during most of 1990.

At successive board meetings in the chairman's office in Scunthorpe during late 1990 and into 1991 increasing levels of dissatisfaction were expressed with the volume of sales that were being achieved. All the while the total UK market for tractors continued to fall. For example, July 1991 was down 20.2% compared with the same month in the previous year, and it seemed to be the feeling on the part of some members of the board that now was not a good time to be promoting tractors from a relatively high cost base such as Austria.

To cut costs I was instructed to make first Andy MacMeechan and then Martin Stokes redundant. Shortly afterwards, two of our three workshop personnel who worked on pre-delivery inspections (fitting auto-hitches, front weight frames and cab radios) suffered the same fate. John Coull and Pat McNamarra had worked in Bathgate, John on final inspection and Pat on gearbox assembly. They moved south to work in Britannia Works in Gainsborough, then to Scunthorpe to build tractors there and had been retained to work on the D Series. They were two men with irreplaceable levels of experience.

Martin Stokes and I both joined the Nuffield Organisation – Martin in the service department and myself in sales – on exactly the same day, 1 January 1962.

Some readers may be wondering what happened to Ron Kettle? Ron joined Nuffield when it was based in Longbridge in 1965 and he and I moved to Scunthorpe in 1986 following the demise of the Gainsborough company in September of the previous year. We continued to work together on both UK and export sales until he was offered a directorship in a company set up by two other ex-Marshall Gainsborough employees, who had spotted a good opportunity to compete for a slice of the huge world-wide spare parts business for Nuffield, Leyland and Marshall tractors.

Ron's involvement with the tractor range that had taken him to many of the further flung and, in some cases, less desirable export markets around the world came to an end around 1988 or 1989. Rather than working together, as we had done for nearly a quarter of a century, we were now in competition of sorts.

Two other colleagues were shortly to follow Ron. Rob Mackay had moved down from Bathgate to help set up production in Gainsborough and became a production foreman and eventually moved to Scunthorpe. Cliff Haw, a meticulous office administrator in both Gainsborough and Scunthorpe, was also persuaded to join the new operation.

BELOW LEFT:
The Marshall team in Austria in mid-1989, from left, me, Martin Stokes, managing director Peter Carter, Andy McMeechan and Johan Pienhof, Steyr business manager.

BELOW RIGHT:
Marshall men deep in discussion at the 1990 Royal Highland Show, from left, Andy McMeechan, Andy Lambert, Martin Stokes and me.

While on this particular tack, what about what remained of the production facility for the Leyland/Marshall type range? Well, in truth, the vast bulk of it had already been sold off either by the receivers of the Gainsborough company or by Bentall Simplex when they eventually purchased the business.

Machine tools that had come down from Bathgate and which were specific to the manufacture of the tractor all went prior to the move to Scunthorpe. As a result Scunthorpe was very much a low-volume, assembly-type operation and there was very little of a material consequence that remained when the decision was made to go down the road of badge engineering with Steyr.

What did remain was a small band of highly experienced men whose future now looked more and more uncertain – in particular there was Harold Jubb and Dave (Sid) Brown, who knew the assembly of the Gainsborough-built 100-4 tractor inside out.

Marshall Daimler still owned the intellectual property rights to the Nuffield, Leyland and Marshall designs. It was realised that other manufacturers had not merely buried old designs when the time had come for them to be superseded. Perhaps there was something to be gained from selling our designs to another company?

A brief and fruitless series of dialogues took place with Belarus but in the end it was a combination of enthusiasm for and dedication to the product coupled with a desire to keep it in British ownership plus, it has to be said, hard-headed business appreciation that saw the transfer of ownership of the production rights and considerable quantities of componentry to one of our dealers, J. Charnley & Sons of Brindle, near Chorley, Lancs. This company went on to introduce a version of the old Marshall tractor under the JWD Fieldmaster name and it has also established a world-wide reputation for the supply of parts for Nuffield, Leyland and Marshall.

As I recall, it was some time in late August of 1991 that the chairman had a meeting with Steyr at which it was decided that the agreement between the two companies should be terminated. As sales director I was asked to inform the dealers of this decision and a general letter was mailed on 10 September 1991.

The letter read: 'With the continuing decline in the size of the UK tractor market we have been reviewing, together with Steyr, our competitive position in the market place.

Steyr have seen a considerable improvement in their sales figures into the UK as a result of the sales and marketing agreement with Marshall and are, therefore, not unhappy with the present situation. However, we for our part are not satisfied with the sales volumes we have been able to achieve during the last 12 months. This is no reflection on the Austrian sourced product but is simply the result of our not being prepared, together with Steyr, to compete with the commercially unviable levels of price cutting and discounting being thrust upon the market place by a high proportion of our competitors.

In this situation we have decided that sales volumes cannot profitably be raised to the levels needed by Marshall Daimler Ltd. As a result, we have mutually agreed with Steyr that the agreement between our two companies is terminated.'

The letter concluded by saying: 'We would like to express our thanks and appreciation to those main dealers who have shown commitment to and have been active in the sale of the Steyr based D Series Marshall Tractors.'

The last D Series was dispatched from Scunthorpe in August 1991 to Timothy McFarland. It was also the last time that the famous Marshall name would appear on the bonnet of a new tractor. The Leyland/Marshall marque had experienced a long and slow decline ever since British Leyland's tractor division became the first part of the state-owned company to be privatised in late 1981. But it was not just a fine range of British tractors that had disappeared – it was also a large team of hard working, experienced, dedicated and enthusiastic men and women.

As for Tony Thomas, I had been fortunate to have worked with some tremendously talented people and with one product range for almost 30 years. I was in my mid-50s and tractors and agriculture were, from an employment point of view, just about all I knew. I also knew that following the brief encounter with the Steyr range, and the fact that we no longer had a tractor division, my services would not be required by my employers for much longer, and so it proved to be.

LEFT:
Marshall dealers inspect the new D-Series tractors at the launch at Nottingham University. Some embraced the new models, while others relinquished their franchises.

BELOW LEFT:
The mid-range Marshall D844 model (22 units) accounted for over 25% of the total sales of D-Series tractors between late 1989 and mid-1991.

BELOW RIGHT:
Marshall's S-Series models had a basic level of specification and low-profile cabs. This S-544 RS2 was sold new by dealer T. Parker & Sons of Surrey.

Epilogue

One thing you pick up along the way while working for companies large and small is a great degree of resilience and versatility. The sales and marketing skills that I gained with Nuffield, Leyland and Marshall stood me in good stead during the final ten years of my working life, when I operated a franchise for the whole-sale distribution of – wait for it – greetings cards. And that is a multi-million pound market in which the UK is a world leader!

While reading the story of my 30 years with the Nuffield, Leyland and Marshall tractor companies, I am sure you will have noticed frequent references to the sad demise, as I see it, of the British tractor manufacturing industry.

So before signing off, I'm sure you'll forgive me for taking one last brief look back at what we, as a nation and as the Nuffield, Leyland and Marshall companies, achieved as a major exporter of tractors.

The time was, during the 1960s, 70s and even into the 80s, when this country exported more tractors than the rest of the world put together. In short, we were the major world supplier of agricultural tractors. There were five major brands: Ford, Massey Ferguson, David Brown, International Harvester and Nuffield, which in 1969 became Leyland, each with at least one manufacturing base dotted around the UK. In addition there were several smaller, specialist manufacturers such as County, Roadless and Muir-Hill.

When I joined the Nuffield Tractor division of the British Motor Corporation on 1 January 1962 the market for new tractors in the UK was around 40,000 units per year. Virtually every one of them would have been manufactured in one of the factories owned by the above-mentioned companies. Additionally, many hundreds of thousands of tractors would have been produced in those same factories for export all over the world.

From records that I still have, the year 1960 saw 146,287 tractors exported and in terms of value to our balance of payments they were worth £86mn. In the same year Nuffield produced just over 9400 tractors, Ford 71,500 and MF also 71,500. In 1962, the Nuffield tractor was being built at Ward End, Birmingham. In common with the factories responsible for the manufacture of its four main competitors, between 75% and 80% of the units that came off the end of the production line were destined to go abroad.

The Nuffield factory was small by comparison with the plants of Ford, MF and International Harvester. Even following the opening of the Bathgate factory in Scotland, production figures did not match these three makes and they just about equaled those of the David Brown factory at Meltham. Even so, tractor manufacturing as a whole was a hugely important industry and it generated many £millions in export earnings.

How things have changed and how we, as a nation, have lost out. Whereas British designed and built tractors once ploughed most of the world, we now rely on tractors built beyond these shores to plough our own fields!

Talking of fields, most of us are now out to grass in our retirement and some of those I have mentioned are sadly no longer with us and the list of these people grows inexorably longer. It includes the names of great, knowledgeable, dedicated and hard working personalities such as Martin Stokes, Andy McMeechan, Dominic McClafferty, Bob Turner, Val Muir, Mike Barnes, John Coull, John Mill, Rob Mackie and John Cubbin. There are probably others but with the passage of time it becomes increasingly difficult to maintain contact. On a brighter note and mid-way through 2012, many of the old team are still active, to varying degrees! Brian Webb has recently retired, well almost, and keeps himself busy farming in a small way with a Leyland 262 Synchro as his main source of power, as well as following both football and cricket.

Ron Kettle still lives close to Gainsborough and has a largish garden and green house to occupy himself; Alan Hawes has recently retired following a very long stint in the tractor industry, latterly with New Holland; while Ray Runciman is also now a gentleman of leisure. Ray became managing director of Collings Bros of Abbotsley Ltd in 1984, so his period in the industry is about the same length as Alan's. John Paterson, who worked for a British Leyland subsidiary in Nigeria for a time following the closure of Bathgate, is also retired and among other things runs the website for the Nuffield & Leyland Tractor Club. I am also in contract with other former colleagues such as Brian Sneyd, Julian Bown, Keir Wyatt, Jim Lavendar, John Arkell, George Livingstone, Ian Jack, Aiden Kendall and Peter Hitchens.

The Nuffield & Leyland Tractor Club is so ably and enthusiastically organised and run by Pam Harlow and Graham Towndrow. Many of us are already members of the club and it is strongly recommended to those with an interest in the products of Nuffield, Leyland and Marshall.

Almost 50 years after we appeared with 701 UJO on the cover of the Nuffield 10/42 and 10/60 sales brochure, Brian Webb, left, and I were reunited with the tractor, which now belongs to Malcolm Williams, centre, at Tractor World at Malvern in 2012.